publishing photography

publishing photography

Dewi Lewis & Alan Ward

Cornerhouse Publications
•
Manchester

First published in 1992
by Cornerhouse Publications
70 Oxford Street
Manchester M1 5NH
061 228 7621

ISBN 0 948797 81 9
British Library Cataloguing-in-Publication Data.
A Catalogue record for this book is available from the British Library.

Cover Design: Axis Design, Manchester
Typesetting & Artwork: Niall Allsop/Cornerhouse Production
Print: Alden Press, Oxford

acknowledgements

Many people have helped me over the five years in which I have been attempting to get to grips with photographic publishing. I have made many good friends in publishing and I would like to thank them all for giving so generously of their time and their knowledge.

I would particularly like to thank Alison Buchan, who as the other founding half of Cornerhouse Publications has contributed beyond measure to our success. Without her determination, her expertise and her total commitment our plans would have withered and died.

And of course all the photographers, writers, designers and printers with whom we have worked. I would also thank Alan Ward who has not only worked as designer on a number of our books but has also contributed to this book by writing the section on design. And finally Stephanie Laidler for coping with so much of the typing and proofing for this book.

preface

I have yet to meet the photographer who doesn't want to see their work in book form. Few will achieve that goal, many will find the process of getting into print frustrating to the point of desperation. It is not easy and it is certainly not for the faint-hearted.

There are many books that use photographs for illustration but very few that attempt to use photography as a medium of visual communication in its own right. Many publishers have at one time or another published what might be termed a serious photography book. Most have not repeated their attempt, deciding that photography books are quite simply not a viable proposition. Even at the international level there are few publishers specialising in photography books and those that do so are frequently established either as not-for-profit organisations or are supported by committed individuals using income generated from other sources. To produce good quality photographic books is both expensive and risky and as a consequence commercial viability is evasive.

This book is intended as an introduction to photographic publishing. It is, I hope, a reasonably comprehensive guide for those seeking to act as self-publishers in their own right, but it is also intended to better prepare photographers in their quest for publication at a general level.

I have tried to present practical information and advice and I hope that the sections at the back of the book will provide useful reference material. The subject of publishing is massive and of neccesity there is much that I have had to pass over, not least because there is still much that I have to learn. I have tried to focus my attention on those elements which are likely to be most helpful to a photographer rather than confuse and confound by exploring in more than outline detail such things as the technological developments in desk top publishing or printing. There are many excellent books which cover these areas and which those interested may wish to consult. I have provided suggestions for further reading and I can only stress that time spent in preliminary research will be more than repaid. There will never be any guarantee that your work will be published, or indeed that it is publishable, but you will have at least given yourself the best possible chance.

As I have suggested some photographers will wish to consider acting as their own publishers – as self-publishers. This is not vanity publishing but a valid and worthwhile approach that should not be dismissed. A number of well known photographers have adopted this strategy with great success. Both Martin Parr and Paul Graham, for example, published a number of their early books themselves and were able to create excellent publications that contributed significantly to the development of Britsh Photography in the 1980s. Specific schemes for grant-aid support are available through the funding bodies such as the Arts Council and some of the RegionalArts Boards. There are also many examples of sponsorship being raised as a substantial contribution towards publication costs.

Whichever route you seek to follow I have no doubt that it will be hard. I hope that this book will in some small measure ease that route and encourage you on the way. If it helps to bring out even one good photography book it will have done its job.

Dewi Lewis
July 1992

contents

the book business

Many of us still carry a romantic notion of the bookshop. We see it as somewhere we will find a copy of J.R.Hartley's "Fly-Fishing" hidden amongst dusty shelves filled with volumes of wonderment. For us bookshops are repositories of human knowledge and experience, a world away from the supermarket and its shelves brimming with baked beans and spaghetti hoops. Bookshops have an intellectual vigour about them and of course they would all wish to stock our particular book if only we could find a publisher.

The reality is of course very different. Books have very largely become products like any other retail product. Few, if any, bookshops can afford to keep stock that doesn't sell reasonably quickly. A fast turnover is as important a factor in bookshops as it is in any other retail outlet selling similarly priced goods. There are still bookshops where the love of books is the primary motive for the bookshop owner but it is perhaps realistic to recognise that these are increasingly the exceptions that prove the rule.

We still talk about "good" bookshops, meaning those that are stocked to the roof, with all those fascinating titles that we want to browse through with little intention of buying. I would love to see them long continue but I doubt that I will. The success of a bookshop is now more frequently measured in financial ratios; sales per square foot; sales per employee; stock turn; return on capital employed. Bookselling has truly become a business.

And so it is with publishers – we romanticise. For me two images spring to mind. The "gentleman" publisher – ensconced in a mahogany panelled office, shelves full of beautifully tooled leather volumes, the decanter on the side; and the media mogul – the Maxwell, the Murdoch – the focus of personal and professional communication networks that span the globe. The one apparently determining cultural life, the other arguably determining political life. Both models may exist – the latter certainly does – but they are not a true reflection of publishing. It is ultimately an industry, much like any other.

During the eighties publishing went through major changes. Small companies were swallowed up by larger ones and those in their turn were swallowed up by even larger conglomerates and multi-nationals. The bottom line became the prime motive as many publishers espoused a strategy where product became subservient to profit. None of this is particularly surprising, simply a manifestation of the *zeitgeist* of the decade – the Thatcher years.

what is publishing?

It is perhaps easiest to think about the different tasks that a publisher might have to undertake.

* Finding projects which might work in book form

   Research is an important role for the publisher. Whilst many unsolicited proposals will be received the majority of these are likely to be unsuitable for taking forward. It is therefore important for any publisher to develop their own network of contacts and if they are publishing in a specialist area to keep abreast of key developments and key figures in that area.

* Developing and refining those projects

   Very few proposals arrive in a form or at a stage which is suitable for publication. A publisher will take on an editorial role and will seek to work closely with the author or photographer to refine the proposal and make it more appropriate to the book form. In terms of a photographic book the publisher may wish to see an accompanying text and may explore possible writers in consultation with the photographer.

* Preparing them for production

   It is the responsibility of the publisher to appoint the designer and determine the printer most suitable for the project. I have always taken the view that the choice of designer on a photographic book should be mutually agreed with the photographer. It is one of the areas of publishing in which the ability of the designer to grasp the concept and direction of the project is most important. As a visual presentation of work it is essential to ensure that there is no conflict in the visual ideas of these two contributors.

Once the approach has been agreed the publisher takes on responsibility for ensuring that the artwork is provided in the form required by the printer. The publisher may also take on an editorial role in relation to any accompanying text and will take responsibility for proofreading and typesetting.

- Supervising all the stages of production

Whilst we encourage our photographers to be actively involved in the supervision of the production process the ultimate responsibility lies with the publisher. We must try to balance the needs of the printer with the wishes of the photographer. We must aim for the perfect book and aim for the highest standards that we can achieve. As the publisher, however, we will inevitably be aware of cost and of the compromises that may be necessary to achieve commercial viability.

- Financing the production

Even if you could sell every copy of a book before publication you would still be unlikely to receive your income before you have to pay out the costs of production. The publisher provides access to the finance necessary to undertake the book and of course takes the financial risk in the event of the book being a sales failure.

- Marketing the book to the book-buying public

It is hard work producing a photography book but harder work selling it. There are two processes in this. We must persuade the customers to buy the title but we must first persuade the bookshops to stock it.

Marketing the book to the public is clearly important but it serves little purpose unless you are also having a direct impact on the bookshops.

- Selling the book to the retail outlets

  Selling to the shops really requires direct contact and this is why
  sales reps play a significant role in the book trade. They visit their
  major accounts at regular intervals showing new titles and trying to
  encourage the reordering of titles on the backlist. Publishers will
  have a sales force operating in many parts of the world who will
  need to be kept in close contact and regularly informed about the
  company's publishing programme if they are to be most effective.

- Distributing it to those outlets

  It is important for bookshops that titles can be supplied speedily.
  Increasingly shops carry smaller stocks and rely heavily on publishers
  and wholesalers being able to offer fast order fulfilment.

- Receiving and accounting for the income generated

  Having sold the book we obviously then have to collect payment.
  When sales are made internationally as is the case for most publishers
  this is not an easy task. Delays in payment and bad debts are a
  recurrent problem.

  Finally we must ensure that we keep proper records of all sales to
  enable correct royalty payments to be made to our photographers.

A publisher plays many roles. In a large publishing house you would
expect to find each of these areas of work split across different
departments and undertaken by staff with highly specialised expertise.
With a small publisher all the tasks may, at most, be the responsibility
of a handful of people, and often of only one or two.

Publishing is a complex industry and as such has evolved a complex
range of trade and distributive practices. On the surface the process of
selling books appears to be a simple one. It may be, but it certainly is
multi-faceted. As an industry, publishing relies heavily on a large
number of service organisations offering elements of a marketing,
sales and distribution package. Publishers inevitably undertake at
least some level of marketing to establish awareness of a title. For large
publishers this may extend to media and press campaigns and will
often utilise the services of specialist PR companies, for smaller
publishers the marketing strategy may be limited to printed catalogues

and extensive attempts to encourage reviews and other forms of editorial coverage.

This is then followed up by sales reps who will present a title to the relevant book-buyer at the retail outlet. Whilst large companies do employ their own sales force many reps operate on a freelance basis carrying a number of compatible publisher's lists. They will have a pre-defined geographical area. For those that are freelance much of their income will be generated through commission and they will therefore be totally reliant on their ability to sell from the lists they carry. The lack of overhead cost is an attraction to publishers but balancing this is the reality that the reps will push hardest for those titles and publishers which can generate the greatest financial return. There may also be a tendency to service the larger retail outlets in preference to those whose total purchases might be relatively small. Consequently it can be difficult for the smaller specialist publisher to establish good market penetration.

Distribution is the next link in the chain. Again it is serviced by a range of companies offering everything from storage and physical distribution only, through to a comprehensive service also covering invoicing and credit control and incorporating sales representation. The smaller publishers inevitably face the problem that they can only offer a limited financial return to any service provider. They simply do not sell sufficient books to be an attractive proposition to commercial distributors. Consequently they are likely to pay higher percentage charges and they may also find that minimum turnover levels are set which they are not able to achieve.

Perhaps the overriding restriction, however, is cost. A comprehensive sales and distribution service is a major expense to a small publisher and after including trade discounts can account for some 55% – 60% of the retail price.

the net book agreement

At some point in your search for publication you will come across the phrase "The Net Book Agreement" and no doubt you will be suitably confused. It is a trade agreement which provides that books coming under its terms should not be sold at less than the publisher's stated list price. In essence its supporters argue that it provides a protection for the smaller bookshop against the larger chains which through an aggressive discounting policy could distort control of the trade. Over recent years the arguments and counter arguments for and against the NBA seem to have been endless. Nothing has really changed yet but it is worth noting that there is increasingly a view that the NBA will not survive as an effective mechanism for much longer. A number of bookshops, with Dillons at the forefront, have begun to challenge it and at the same time an increasing number of publishers have begun to exclude certain titles from the NBA status.

In the last year the Net Book Agreement has looked increasingly vulnerable. A recent decision in the European Court has led to immediate changes in certain of the restrictions being applied particularly those which impact in any way on the other member states of the EEC. This setback is being read by many as the first step in the dismantling of the NBA. Within the NBA certain discounts can be offered but these are strictly limited.

- Schools can apply for a licence from the Publishers Association which will enable them to buy from the trade at a 10% discount.

- Libraries can nominate a supplier and apply for a library licence. This entitles them to a 10% discount.

- Books can be supplied by a retailer to "book agents" to enable bookstalls and the like to be run by schools and other organisations. A licence is again required.

- Other discount opportunities include a quantity book-buying licence, and the National Book Sale during which bookshops may discount on any stock that they have held for more than a year.

For the self-publisher there is the decision as to whether to make a book net or non-net. It is very much dependent on the way in which you plan to sell. If you want to work through the trade then it is best to go net, but if you intend to sell almost exclusively via mail order, perhaps because you are appealing to a specialist and reachable market, then non-net is probably most appropriate. Be warned that if your book is non-net then shops may not discount it but may increase the price above the level that you have suggested. Clearly this can be expected to impact on sales.

profiling the booksellers

In 1985 consultants Arthur Young undertook a report for the Booksellers Association (*The Demand for Books*) which estimated the market shares of the principal distribution channels. To my knowledge this still remains the most up to date detailed survey. It showed a split as follows

Specialist Bookshops	30%
WH Smith	20%
Book Clubs	10%
Newsagents/CTNs	16%
Supermarkets	3%
Department Stores	2%
Variety Stores	7%
Others	12%

Between 1985 and 1989 a total of 746 new bookshops opened. In 1990 The Booksellers Association, which is the primary trade organisation, had 3,109 members in the United Kingdom. Since then there have also been many closures with the smaller independent bookshops being frequent victims of the recessionary pressures of the last 18 months.

Over recent years there have also been changes in ownership with WH Smith now also controlling the Waterstones and Sherratt & Hughes chains. These two chains are estimated to share just under 10% of the consumer market. Grouped together therefore it would be realistic to anticipate the share of the market now held by WH Smith being close to 30%. However if you looked at it another way and discounted the book clubs and what could be termed as the non-specialist retail outlets then it can be argued that the real impact of that overall market share may be as high as 60% of the outlets that most people would recognise as bookshops.

Whilst Waterstones and Sherratt & Hughes operate very much as traditional bookshops, WH Smith itself operates in a highly centralised manner using central buying as a significant part of its purchasing policy. For the smaller publisher this leads to far greater difficulties in getting books in to their shops. The managers themselves do have a degree of purchasing flexibility in terms of "local" books and if your title can be projected in this way it is well worth an approach.

Over recent years another factor has also been significant in reducing the range of stock available through bookshops – electronic stock control linked to the growth of wholesalers. Keeping track of the thousands of books published in the UK each year is a daunting task for booksellers. It is now possible to purchase your stock almost exclusively by working through one or two wholesale accounts. For the smaller bookshop this can save considerably on the administration time spent, particularly in the monitoring of hundreds of individual accounts with which the bookshops previously dealt. It can also mean that they are able to be kept advised of the books that are selling well in other shops and adjust their own stock levels accordingly. The downside is very much one of a more limited range for the customer.

The larger wholesalers generally limit their range to no more than 50 – 60,000 titles, the smaller ones considerably less, and tend not to look that favourably on the lists of the smaller publishers. The reasons are very understandable.

- A limited stock range is easier to control.

- Limiting the number of suppliers simplifies administration.

- Smaller publishers do not have the marketing budgets for their books to ensure that they will get good exposure to the general public.

- Creating larger purchase accounts helps ensure that better discount structures can be agreed.

A stock of 50,000 titles may sound a lot but when you view it alongside the number of books currently in print (estimated at some 500,000) it is daunting to realise that some 90% of available books are not considered core stock.

book clubs

Book clubs are an important feature of the UK book market. It is interesting to note that the Arthur Young report showed their market share as 10% (*The Demand for Books*, 1985). This is a very high share of a retail market for mail order operations. Translated into unit terms this suggests a massive 50 million books retailed through this approach.

Whilst art and photography books play a role in this, the type of books sold tend to be generally mainstream titles and it is rare for the smaller publisher to break into this market effectively.

Book Clubs are strictly governed through the Publishers Association which keeps a register of clubs and controls the terms that can be offered to members. Essentially these controls are imposed to ensure that the Net Book Agreement is not unfairly circumvented. The regulations mean that members must make a minimum purchasing commitment though in recent years some flexibility has been introduced to this. Books which are non-net are outside the agreement and therefore any specialist club offering non-net books is free to determine its own terms and conditions.

The advantages of the book club structure are based on the ability of the clubs to offer a mail order service that discounts sales to their members. A number of organisations, commercial and subsidised, have sought to develop mail order without this discount structure – Portfolio Gallery in Edinburgh and The Photographers' Gallery in London are two such examples from the subsidised sector. Success has been hard to achieve. There are a number of reasons.

- When only limited discounting is possible (on imported books and others falling outside the NBA) the real cost to the customer, after postage and packing costs, is higher than if they had made their purchase by placing a customer order with a bookshop. For those customers who have reasonable access to a bookshop that will accept customer orders, this removes much of the incentive.

- People feel that they would like to see what they are buying. The book clubs generally try to get around this by offering full return facilities on the books that they supply. The inertia principle then comes into operation. If customers are reasonably satisfied it is easier for them to hold on to the book than to return it, particularly as they would have to pay the return postage cost.

- Mail order operations need proper financial and staffing resources. List building and customer base development requires a lot of staff time for little initial return.

new models for bookselling

The sales processes for video, cards and records are essentially very similar to that of books. However, they rarely operate in exactly the same circles. The image of the Olympic symbol with its inter-relating rings is an appropriate metaphor. Whilst there is overlap in outlets selling across this range of goods it still remains relatively small. There is evidence of a shift in product range in many shops and this will increasingly provide opportunities for publishers and other producers seeking to diversify. In recent years some bookshops have begun to explore the potential for such sales and have even committed themselves to such developments. Volume One bookshops (owned by the Goldstein brothers creators of the SuperDrug chain) announced last year that it was to allocate around 25% of its trading area to the sale of video. Another example of this approach is the Heffers paperback and video shop in Cambridge.

There are many other examples of a new approach to bookselling both in this country and in Europe. The FNAC chain (in France and Belgium) is not only a significant bookseller but also a major outlet for music and for video. The combination works well. The shops are large, well-stocked and immensely busy. They feature an exhibition space which is used for photographic exhibitions and a film processing service is also offered. There are similarities in approach between FNAC and the Virgin super stores. Whilst Virgin currently offer only limited bookselling, and that targeted at a primarily youth market, their increased involvement in publishing in their own right suggests that they recognise a base compatibility in these areas of operation. I would suggest that there is potential in the UK for a large operator to further develop this sort of model.

arts publishing in the united kingdom

The Arts Council of Great Britain and the Regional Arts Boards have over the years taken an active role in funding publishing. They have not only provided support towards production costs but have also allocated funding to distributors to encourage the development of services to art, photography and literary publishers. This has certainly proved beneficial giving some access to distribution networks for a number of self-publishers and small-scale producers. There is, however, considerable evidence that the system functions inadequately. Whilst it can provide an initial access to the distribution chain it has often done so in a way that still marginalises the product. Many bookshops are inherently suspicious of "arts" publications and this view can be reinforced unless the contact with the shops is a convincing and professional one. Professional sales staff are therefore needed but they must also have sufficient incentive to present these "arts" titles effectively. Linking to existing commercially based sales and distribution systems provides the professionalism but as yet no system of effective incentive has been provided. This is an area that needs urgent consideration if it is not to impact critically on the longer term development potential of arts publishing in the UK.

catalogues and gallery publications

Catalogues have an important role to play in marking the shifts of visual culture.

Galleries have a range of motives for the production of catalogues. The apparent similarity of a catalogue to a book is generally misleading and inappropriate. The purpose may be one of documentation of an essentially ephemeral event (ie the exhibition); it may be seen as a form of payment to the artist; it may form part of the corporate image development for the gallery, useful as an approach device to potential sponsors for a future unrelated exhibition. These are all clearly valid and valuable reasons for going into print but they should not be confused with commercial intent.

In general insufficient thought is given to considerations of commercial viability and return. Over-optimism is however frequently present. Despite the evidence of very limited sales potential for catalogues, at all but the major national galleries, galleries continue to over-produce. Store rooms throughout the UK testify to this. The unit cost of 2,000 catalogues is certainly less than that of 500 but the total cost of 500 is still lower. If that is the likely market then that is the number that should be produced.

Galleries have specific problems in relation to access to any effective distribution chain. Production is often infrequent; print runs are too low, and consequently unit costs too high, to enable resources to be dedicated to any marketing operation. Yet taken at a national level the resources committed by galleries to catalogues are significant.

It is unrealistic to believe that galleries individually will be able to make any significant impact in the distribution of their catalogues. If it is believed that catalogues have a significance then intervention is needed by the funding bodies to ensure adequate methods of distribution. It is clear from increasing gallery attendances that there is an interested and committed audience. The question is how to harness this interest most effectively. This is a concern that continues to exercise not only the galleries but also the funding bodies. If the existing distribution networks for visual arts publications can be effectively supplemented then there is little doubt that photographic books will also feel the benefit. I watch this space with great interest.

looking at statistics

The Publishers Association's *"Book Publishing in the United Kingdom – Key Facts 1990"* offers significant trade information on the UK Publishing Industry.

In 1989 61,195 titles were published by British Publishers. Of these 46,042 were new titles as opposed to reprints or new editions. 1,481 were categorised as Art books – some 2.5% of the total.

The 1989 UK home market for books was £2.4bn at retail prices with a further £642m being generated through export sales. Publishing is clearly an international trade and whilst the overall export sales percentage is high, at just over 20%, the export market for specialist publishers such as Cornerhouse can be considerably higher.

Some 500 million books were sold in the year giving an average of some nine books per person – this makes the UK one of the highest book buying publics in the world. In addition the public libraries system is estimated to have made a further nine loans per person – another 500 million in all.

Quite understandably the book market mirrors social and political trends. The number of consumer books sold in 1989 was 450 million, increasing by 15% from the 390 million sold in 1981. Academic books (24m) increased by 31% partially explained by increases in student numbers, whilst school books (31m) declined by 33%, reflecting quite clearly the stringent public spending controls being exerted. Overall there was an increase over the period of 11% with maximum sales being achieved at the height of the economic boom in 1986.

In real (inflation adjusted) terms, sales of all books increased in value by 38% between 1981 and 1989 – a growth of some 4% a year above inflation. At the same time consumer book prices maintained parity with inflation, suggesting that during the period there was a tendency on the part of the consumer towards buying higher value books.

Despite the relatively buoyant market during the larger part of the eighties bookselling remained on average less profitable than retailing in general. The 1988/9 figures showed a return on turnover of 3.3% as compared to 6.6% for UK retailers as a whole. The return on capital employed was also comparatively poor. In 1988/9 it ran at 11.8% as compared to 18.4% for UK retailers as a whole. Whilst this can be partly explained by the significant increases in the capital being invested into bookshop developments at the time bookshops have historically performed less well than the retail sector as a whole. (Source: *ICC Industrial Performance Analysis*).

Official surveys continue to show that book readership by UK adults is increasing. *The General Household Survey* showed an increase between 1977 to 1987 from 54% of the population reading a book in a four week period to 60%. This was further confirmed by the *Government's Family Expenditure Survey* which showed a 34% increase on expenditure on books (after adjusting for inflation) between 1981 and 1989.

who buys books?

The profile of book buyers was assessed by the British Market Research Bureau in a study for the Publishers Association's Book Marketing Council. The following key points emerged as identifying those termed "heavy buyers".

• They are most likely to be found in the middle age groups – two-thirds of them are aged 25-54.

• They are likely to have children.

• They are likely to be better educated with almost half having continued their education beyond 16.

- They are likely to enjoy higher than average incomes.

- There is a clear bias towards the south of England.

No real surprises here but useful nonetheless in confirming the type of marketing direction that is most likely to reap dividends. Statistics and trade information are of course most useful to the larger publishers aiming to sell a consumer product. For the specialist publisher with a real commitment to their books the approach will be different. It will not be targeted towards mass market appeal but will instead seek to find its own particular niche. This is always the challenge and ultimately the satisfaction.

understanding the trade

It seems obvious to suggest that anyone either trying to get their work published or to publish it themselves should do as much as they can to gain some understanding of the book trade and should certainly have looked at some of the more recently published photography books. I do, however, frequently get the impression that many photographers submitting book proposals to us last visited a bookshop whilst clutching the five shilling book token that their grandmother had bought them for Christmas.

If you have ever worked in a bookshop then you have a head start. Like most things the book trade is most easily understood from inside. A sensible place to begin, therefore, has to be your local bookshop. The staff may know nothing whatsoever about photography books but they will be a mine of information on the more practical aspects of books and publishing. Of course, if you can get access to a shop that has a more specialist attitude to photography books then do so. Study the shelves to see what is being stocked, who is publishing which sort of books, what the prices are – and ask which ones are selling.

Another place to visit is your local library. They will almost certainly have at least a few titles on the subject of publishing and you could also ask if there was someone who could tell you about libraries – how they buy and what it is that interests them.

I would also suggest that you get hold of copies of "The Bookseller", the trade's weekly magazine. Again this is a mine of information, much of it apparently not directly relevant, but actually excellent in giving you an overall picture of what motivates and drives the trade.

However, if you are really serious about publishing a book then you should take the intensive study course – visit one of the major bookfairs.

frankfurt book fair

Every year around the beginning of October the publishing industry packs its bags and begins the mass exodus to Frankfurt. Small publishers, large publishers; publishers from Canada and Chile, Italy and India; designers, distributors; authors, artists; they all pack the aisles of the immense Frankfurt Messe – the fairground.

Frankfurt is an education. In the six gruelling days that it runs you can learn more about the state of world publishing than you would in a lifetime of reading about it. With its several thousand stands it covers the best and the worst of the book world. Booksellers come in their droves bussed in from all parts of Germany and from neighbouring countries. Many of the larger international booksellers also fly in for this publishing circus. And even the book-buying public are allowed in, though this is much to the chagrin of the publishers themselves.

Frankfurt is primarily seen as a Rights Fair. It is there for publishers to haggle over the rights for the latest, yet to be published, blockbuster by a well-known author or the next exposé of the royal family, and to set up co-edition deals. It is also a magnificent opportunity to meet old friends and make new contacts, to review successes and failures and explore new ways of working.

We first went to Frankfurt in 1988. With a grant from the DTI and all the confidence that comes from ignorance we put on display our magnificent range of titles – four in all. We were of course surrounded by publishers with enough titles on display on their stands to be able to stock a small branch library. We had, however, taken great pains to think about the design of our stand, thanks to Chris Lord who was the Cornerhouse in-house designer at the time. The result was very effective and counterbalanced our lack of stock with an immense amount of style. I have since managed to ignore remarks about all style no substance.

Looking back I have to admit that we didn't sell many books that first time but through the things we learned I'm sure that we speeded up the development of Cornerhouse Publications by at least two to three years. For six days I walked the aisles talking to anyone who would talk and showing our books to anyone who would look at them. A lot of people came to our stand but more out of curiosity than a real interest in photography, that is apart from the many photographers showing their wares and desperate to find a publisher at least willing to give them the time of day.

We went back the next year and have returned every year since. At our third fair in 1990 and more so in 1991, however, we began to notice that a change was taking place. Suddenly we were being chased by people rather than the other way around. Sales reps wanted to represent us, wholesalers wanted to talk terms, publishers wanted to meet to talk through deals, and of course the number of photographers wanting to show work just kept on growing.

Frankfurt is not to be faced with a new pair of shoes. Well-worn, solid and comfortable ones are as essential as stamina and perseverance. I always recommend that anyone interested in publishing their work should try to get over to Frankfurt for at least three days starting with the opening day. However, be warned, hotel rooms double their prices during the fair. They are also incredibly difficult to find. If you leave your booking any later than the Easter before the fair you will find it almost impossible to book a room in advance and will have to take the chance of finding one on the spot. There is a hotel booking service at the airport and they will do their utmost to find you something if you arrive without any accommodation. It may be up to an hour away from the city centre.

If you want to show your work to potential publishers then follow this strategy:

- Get hold of a copy of the Fair catalogue in advance. Check through it and mark up all the publishers that you want to see. Make a list in priority order.

- Write or fax all the publishers on your list and ask for an appointment. Outline very briefly the work that you want to show.

- Be there on the first day of the fair at opening time.

- Find where your listed publishers are located. Go to their stands as soon as possible and either check to confirm the appointment that has already been made or ask if you can book an appointment to show work.

- While you are moving around the hall keep a look-out for other potential publishers. Add them to your list and return to them in priority order.

- Always stick to your priority listing. If you don't set up your appointments quickly you may find that the publishers have no time left for you.

- Do not expect more than 10-15 minutes at most with each publisher. Many will grant you no more than a few minutes and will flick through your portfolio at what can appear to be an insulting pace. You must realise that many publishers will be holding meetings at quarter hour intervals throughout the day for the full six days. The first two days are the best for appointments simply because later in the week people are beginning to get very tired and more irritable. By day three almost everyone is complaining of a sore throat or sinus problems – such is Frankfurt.

- Be prepared. Know what you are going to say about the work and say it quickly and precisely.

- Present the work in a form that can be viewed easily. A book dummy is perfect. Slides are next to impossible – the light in the exhibition halls is uneven and no-one will have a viewer. Large exhibition prints are just as bad. Avoid anything which is unwieldy. If someone can't sit down just at a chair without a table and look through comfortably then you may have a problem. If you really do want to show large exhibition prints then just show two or three at the end when the publisher has looked through the main body of the work. Bear in mind that whatever you take you will be carrying around for hours and days on end. Do yourself a favour and keep it light.

- Make sure that you keep a note of the name of the person that you have seen and of any comments or suggestions that they have made. Don't be afraid to ask them what their job title is – it may vary from editor to director to vice-president.

- Always leave a card. Ideally use a postcard with one of the images that you have shown, anything larger is a problem for packing. It acts as a very effective aide-memoire. At the end of each Fair I can have literally hundreds of business cards and pieces of paper with names scrawled on them, by which time there are many that are meaningless to me. I have little or no memory of who the people were – photographers, reps, agents, printers, writers, designers – they have all become a blur. The ones I remember most clearly are those that have left something visual.

• When, or rather if, you have run out of publishers to see spend the time looking, talking, listening. Apart from the editors there are a number of people that you should talk to. Don't be afraid of asking what a distributor or a consolidator does if you don't understand the term. A few people may treat you rather rudely but quite a lot will be more than willing to give you a few moments of their time.

the london book fair

The London Book Fair is also worth a visit. Held at Olympia each year usually just before Easter, it is a much smaller affair and much less interesting. But it is worth at least a day of your time. The advice is much the same as for Frankfurt. Try to plan your day so that it will be as effective as possible. Don't just wander around aimlessly – it's very tiring and unproductive – make appointments.

The problem about London is however the size of the fair. It simply doesn't have the range of stands that Frankfurt can offer and as a result there are very few interesting small publishers. It is much more mainstream and although there is an international presence it is limited.

the american booksellers association convention (ABA)

This is the main American bookfair. In size it is a bit of a halfway house between London and Frankfurt and is held in May at a different city each year. Whilst it is an interesting fair with a fascinating mix of publishers it tends to be more geared to bookshop sales than to buying rights or searching out new projects. As with all the fairs though there are always optimistic authors and photographers showing their wares. It is probably only worth a visit if you want to tie it in with a trip to the States or if you feel certain that your book proposal is particularly well-suited to the American market.

We took our first stand at the ABA in Anaheim in 1992 and for us the fair was a great success. Interestingly though our real breakthrough was not in the American market but in the Far East and particularly in Japan – a market that appears to be increasingly interested in European photography.

As I have suggested, if you are trying to get an understanding of the book trade then visiting one of the fairs is an excellent way to do so. If, however, you are at the stage of having prepared a finished book dummy and you are ready to begin touting it around the publishers then London and Frankfurt are a very practical approach to getting the work seen by the right people in a very short time. In a day or so at Frankfurt you should be able to see perhaps close to a dozen publishers. Setting up that number of meetings with a dozen publishers, even if they are all based in the UK, would generally lead to a series of meetings spanning at least a month or two. And if you live outside London the cost of a few days at Frankfurt, though high, will still be considerably less than trekking backwards and forwards to London where, regrettably, the publishing industry is still firmly ensconced.

presenting your work

At Cornerhouse I will in some weeks receive perhaps a dozen unsolicited publication proposals and over a year probably in excess of three hundred. Of these we are unable to give serious consideration to more than twenty. We will eventually publish perhaps two or three of them. The other titles that we will publish in a year coming either from direct approaches that we make to photographers or as a result of discussions with other publishers or galleries with whom we decide to collaborate on a co-production basis. The odds are not good and there are few, if any, signs that they will get much better.

I doubt that we are any different from any other publisher in respect of the large number of proposals that we receive. Against this depressing background how does the relatively unknown photographer, or indeed even the well-known photographer, get a look in? One of the key answers to this is in the way that they present their work.

For me there is no real substitute to presenting the work as a mock-up, or as it is more generally known – a dummy. A dummy is an attempt to show the work in a way that will as closely as possible approximate the finished book. It can take a number of forms which we will look at later.

editing and sequencing

Of course to be able to put together a dummy you must first have established the provisional contents of the book. My experience to date does unfortunately suggest that photographers are not always the best editors of their own work. Innumerable times I have been asked to go and look at work because the photographer says there is too much to send by post. Further questions usually lead me to find that what this means is that there are hundreds of slides or prints on a subject (or more usually several subjects) which have scarcely even been sorted. This type of approach is certain to guarantee some stuttering from me and a polite refusal of the kind invitation. A literary analogy would be for an author to suggest to a publisher that he or she had hundreds of incredible short stories which the publisher could easily make into a best-selling novel. The preliminary edit is the work of the author or the photographer not the publisher.

- Edit your work down to a maximum of 80-90 prints. The majority of photographic books include between 40 and 70 plates. There is unlikely to be any point in offering 200 prints as when production costings are considered this quantity is likely to be unviable. It is also true to say that there are very few photographic projects which are able to sustain a book of this extent.

- Take advice. Not just from other photographers but from anyone who you believe will give an honest assessment of the work.

- Remember that you are preparing a book not an exhibition.

sequencing

A book is not a printed version of an exhibition. It is in every sense an art-form in its own right. Books have an intimacy which I do not believe is possible to recreate in an exhibition. Balancing this, they also have particular limitations. You must therefore always think about sequencing your work in terms of the finished book.

I recommend that at the sequencing stage you should wherever possible try to work with ordinary black and white photocopies. Clearly these will be inferior reproductions of your work but you should know your own work well enough to know what detail is actually in the image and in the case of colour, what the colour balance is.

Having edited your work down to 80 or 90 images and having made photocopies of these you can then lay them out on the floor and begin to try to create a structure to the book.

Sequencing is essentially the exercise of converting single images into a linked "narrative". I take the view that the narrative format is an effective tool in developing a book. Thinking in terms of beginnings, endings and even in terms of chapters helps to develop a flow that gives the work coherence. You should try to vary pace and emphasis and you should also recognise that you are not attempting to gather together "the best of". You are seeking to present an idea, a concept, a view of the world. To do this you will want to play image against image drawing particular attention to some pictures whilst using others as an illustrative support.

At its simplest you will want to play off pictures which are placed on right and left-hand pages. When you start to pair off images you will quickly begin to realise that some pictures sit very uncomfortably on one side or the other. There are photographs which seem quite naturally to be left or right hand page images. But you must think beyond pairing. You must also recognise the way in which an image relates to the one on the preceding or following page.

punctuation

As with text, images need punctuation. Continuous sentences without punctuation may contain the same information but can become almost unintelligible to the reader. The same is true with photographs. Punctuation can take a number of forms. At its simplest it may be the full-stop of the blank page, but equally you should consider using variations in image size, positional placement, grouping or even text itself as ways of breaking up the narrative to make it more comprehensible to the viewer.

book dummies

Book dummies can cost a lot of money to produce or with a little imagination, care and time they can be produced for a few pounds. They can involve a designer but there is no reason why the photographer him or herself can not put one together.

At their most basic they may involve gathering together the set of photocopies running in the page sequence, putting punch holes in each sheet and clipping them together using a file clip, a loose leaf binder or something similar. This is usually my first line of approach when I am undertaking the editing of a book. This is very much the working dummy; a format to allow you to get used to the sequence that you have chosen and one which will allow later changes to be made easily. An alternative to this is to use a Rexel or similar binder. This has transparent pockets in which the images can be placed in the intended sequence. These can look quite professional and can be useful as a preliminary presentation dummy.

Once I am reasonably convinced by the sequence I will then move to a second stage dummy which is intended for presentation. There are several forms of dummy that you can consider.

printer's blank

A Printer's Blank is a properly bound book, either softback or hardback, which comprises blank, unprinted pages. It is made up to the page size that is intended for the finished book and with the same number of pages. It generally uses the same type and weight of paper which is intended for the finished book.

boards or double page spreads

In this approach art-boards to the same size as a double page spread are used. Whilst this allows ease of working the finished result is rather heavy and cumbersome. This approach is often used when a designer has been involved and the quality of artwork presentation is very close to a finished stage. Often no more than ten or so spreads from the book will be presented in this way with the remainder of the images being provided as loose prints or slides.

A variant that I prefer is to use paper rather than boards. These are pasted up again as double page spreads (on one side only) folded to page size and inserted in sequence in a wrap around cover. The effect is much closer to that of the final book.

A further variant of this is used very frequently in the United States. This uses sheets of thin card cut to the size of the single page. These single pages are worked on individually then taped together to form each of the double page spreads. Each page is attached not only to its pair in the double page but also to the page before or after. This creates a continuous concertina of pages and allows the dummy to be read as if it were a finished item. Whilst this form of dummy can look very impressive I find it rather too heavy and bulky and consequently difficult to use.

Colour and laser photocopiers have transformed the ease with which dummies can be produced. Whilst they can not produce facsimile colour they provide a reasonable approximation and are excellent at showing detail particularly in black and white images. They are still expensive though and if at all possible you should try to find somewhere where you can produce your photocopies at cost. This will save some 75% of the cost. This is an area where a little ingenuity and a lot of charm can get you sponsorship in kind. Small sums perhaps but worth trying for.

A well produced book dummy is an achievement in its own right and I would always encourage photographers interested in working in book form to take their work to this stage even if there is very little prospect of getting it published. The discipline that is imposed in the process of editing and sequencing is immensely valuable in understanding how your work is developing and the final object is something that draws that work together, enabling you to see more clearly to what extent you have achieved the objectives that you first set yourself when starting on the project.

Assuming, however, that you have completed your dummy, and are fired up and now doubly committed to getting into print, what should you do next?

Firstly, what to avoid

- Do not approach a publisher unless you have taken the time to research their list and find out whether your project is at all suitable for them. Amongst proposals I have received recently there has been one for a book of poetry, an autobiography, and a how-to book of "glamour" photography. Anyone who had given even a cursory glance at our title list would have realised they were wasting time and money in approaching us with these projects. Suitability does not mean finding a publisher who has already done an almost identical book. What it does mean is to try to identify compatibility between your concept and the intended publisher's editorial approach.

- Do not expect the publisher to fund your world cruise. We receive endless proposals that would involve us in funding extensive travel for the photographer. Interestingly the projects are always in exotic places – Blackburn, Bury and Bognor somehow never feature. As a general rule we do not commission new work. We are looking for proposals which are solidly based on work which has already been started and for which there are sufficient images to show that the objectives are likely to be achieved. Other publishers are also unlikely to finance development unless they know and respect your previous work and are thoroughly convinced of the commercial viability of the project and your ability to deliver.

- Do not expect the publisher to meet with you without having seen some examples of your work. A few will, most won't. If I saw everyone who wanted to show me their portfolio I would spend close to a quarter of my working week doing so. I would also face the very unpleasant job of telling the majority of the 300 photographers that approach us each year that their work was not of interest to us.

- Do not expect a publisher to be overly enthusiastic simply because you have arranged an exhibition of the work. Whilst exhibition is a useful tool in supporting a publication it does not in itself result in significant sales. Our own experience as both an exhibition venue and a publisher is that there are very few galleries that can sell more than fifty copies of book during a five week exhibition period. The importance of exhibition is that it can be used to generate additional press and media coverage and keep the book in the public eye for longer than might otherwise be possible.

- Similarly expect a publisher to be circumspect about any portfolio coverage in the specialist photographic press. If they know their market they are likely to be fully aware of the low circulation of many photographic magazines and as a consequence they will be cautious in their expectations of the sales that are likely to be generated. Even a substantial spread in one of the glossy Sunday supplements will not guarantee sufficient book sales. Publishers will of course be encouraged to find that your work is being favourably received by others. Most people like to feel supported by their peer group in terms of their likes and dislikes.

- Recognise that the time scales for publishing can be fairly protracted. This is partly because of the process itself but it is also because as with any other organisation budgets are determined well in advance.

However strong a project is it may not be possible for a publisher to consider it because they have already made their budgetary commitments.

- Be aware of any time sensitivity in your project. By this I mean that if, for example, your publication proposal ties into the centenary of a major event make your approach in plenty of time. Three years notice makes it very possible, three months does not. On the same point remember that if a subject is currently topical and much discussed it will probably be dead by the time a book comes out. Try to plan ahead and always assume a minimum twelve month run in period.

making the approach

- Research your publishers thoroughly. Get to know their books, look at the way that they approach things, the sort of subjects that appear to interest them.

- Prepare a written outline of your project. Try to summarise it in no more than one or two sides of A4 and keep the description simple and straight forward.

- If you have a background as an established photographer with exhibitions etc, then prepare a CV listing those exhibitions, previous publications, magazine features etc. Again keep it short and don't put in a mass of things simply to fill out the space. If you don't have a track record then your images are going to have to work that little bit harder.

- Prepare an introductory letter drawing attention to any of the key points that you have made in the outline or in your CV. As with the other two items keep it short.

- Make sure that these three items are properly typed and that there are no spelling mistakes.

- Ensure that you have copies of everything including the dummy (or at the very least a proper record of the sequence of images).

- Finally it is a good idea to include some pictures. I always say no more than a dozen. Ensure that they are printed to the same size and that the tonal quality is the same. Don't send very large exhibition prints – 16" x 12" are more than big enough.

- Pack up the dummy safely and neatly. Send it in a reusable box or packing (photographic paper boxes are perfect). Make sure that it is clearly marked with your name and the return address and enclose stamps for the return postage. There is no reason for a publisher to pay for the return of something that they didn't ask for.

- Always send it by registered post or an alternative system that provides proof of delivery.

- In all these areas I have stressed neatness of presentation. It is important. You are asking the publisher to invest a lot of time and money in you and they will want to feel that you are serious and that you are concerned about detail.

- Once you've sent the dummy off do wait two or three weeks before beginning your onslaught on the publisher for their reaction. If you push too hard, too quickly you may just push them to decide too quickly and that decision is more likely to be negative. On the other hand don't sit back and wait for six months for an acknowledgement. If the work isn't of interest to that publisher then you need to be sending it on to someone else. If they are holding it because it has some interest then you want to be arranging a meeting with them as soon as possible.

the appointment

I'm sure that meeting with a publisher for the first time must be a fairly daunting prospect.

- Always phone up the day before to check that the appointment has not been overlooked or that the editor is ill.

- Arrive on time. They may not be able to accommodate your lateness and may have to reschedule the meeting to another day, week or probably month.

- Ensure that any prints you are bringing are again of an even quality and ensure that you have arranged them in the sequence that they appear in the book dummy.

- Expect the meeting to be short. Be ready to talk the editor through the work and try to be sensitive to the speed with which they want to view it.

- Have a list of any questions that you may want to ask. Don't waste time by asking questions that assume that they will do the book until they have said that they will.

- Do ask for the timescale within which they will be able to make their decision.

- If they reject the work ask why and listen to the reasons. You may be able to act on them.

You should always realise that many editors are not in the position to make a publication decision on their own. This is particularly true in the larger companies. An editor may love your work but be unable to persuade the sales and marketing people that there is a market for the project or there may be a competitive book already on sale that is seen as covering the same subject matter. Equally they may run into problems with the production staff who may feel that the production costs are too high to achieve the profit margins that the company has set for itself.

After every meeting with a publisher make notes, both of the positive and negative points made. Ensure that any contacts that they suggest are followed through. If they want you to provide them with any information get back to them as soon as possible whilst your project is still fresh in their minds. Finally, if you are rejected do keep in contact with them if you feel that they are the right sort of publisher for you. By this I mean send invitations to any exhibitions that you are having and make sure that you keep them up to date with any future projects on which you are working.

working with a designer

In most book projects there are three key people involved in the development of the book to the state at which it becomes publishable. There is the photographer, the publisher and the designer. For this section of the book I have asked Alan Ward, who has worked with us on a number of book projects, to outline his views of the role of the designer.

A photographer knows his or her pictures intimately, but the process of putting them together in a coherent, publishable form can be complex. A graphic designer, as a skilled third party, can offer organisational skills and present the visual and written material in an appropriate and interesting format.

There are generally more people involved in the production of a book than just the designer and photographer. There may be writers, publishers, gallery owners and printers, all of whom will want varying levels of involvement. Therefore it is important that a clear working relationship with all the relevant parties is established at an early stage. Each must keep the other fully informed of concept development and progress, budget and production limitations, and deadlines.

The most important relationship in the successful design of a photographic book is that of the designer and the photographer. Both should initially be open to the other's ideas and thoughts with regards to format, image size and typeface. It can be hard to give creative input at an early stage if very strict parameters are set for the designer. Various avenues of thought should be explored before settling on a solution.

The designer should be sympathetic to the context of the work and not be tempted to just apply the contemporary style. Books are an area of design that need to have a certain degree of longevity – a shelf-life. Its form should follow its function. After all, a book of photographic images will generally be admired for its pictorial content. If the design overwhelms and interferes with this, then it is too predominant and unsympathetic.

However, presenting photography in book form, through the careful equation of page, image, text and space, can stimulate other levels of interest in the work. The use of typography can create an additional participation, a visual statement in its own right. Image and text can become a complex layering of ideas that may not be achieved as effectively in gallery space. It is these possibilities that should not be overlooked when exploring ideas with the designer.

The design is clearly important – it should enhance not encroach on the content. The closer the working relationship, especially in the early meetings, the better the chance that this will be reflected in the finished item. If the designer can communicate their complex role and the day to day aspects of the job, the photographer will feel involved with the entire project. An appreciation of deadlines and targets on both sides will help. It is essential that the designer be given all available material at the outset, in order to allow them to make a considered approach from the beginning and not have to compromise or weaken the structure of the design later if additional elements are introduced. Conversely, the photographer should know what is expected regarding visuals, artwork, proofing and production deadlines.

The processes involved in producing a finished bookwork can be broken down into four broad stages:

- Initial briefing (including budget proposals)
- Concept development
- Artwork
- Post-artwork production (including print handling and proofing)

In the initial briefings, describing to the designer what the photographer would like is often difficult. He or she will have ideas and feelings of how it could be and it is important to communicate these to the designer. It may require writers and publishers as well at this stage to give a good overview. Before the designer can make a proper assessment of their input, they will require as much information as possible to do with previously published work, articles, reviews and more specifically the work to be presented in the book: a working set of prints roughly ordered and at least a draft set of the text to be included. The designer should also know at this stage what if any financial limitations there are in order to save wasting time on solutions that can not be produced.

Do not expect the designer to give a quote for the work to be undertaken at this first meeting. They will want to go away and study the information, get typesetting and production quotes and then respond, usually in writing, giving their analysis of the brief and a breakdown of the design fees that will be incurred.

Having completed the above, the designer will produce thumbnail designs for his or her own satisfaction, working on ideas for format and style. It is at this point that considerable time will be spent working on getting the best combination of space, form and size and how that relates to 'A size' presses with regard to paper wastage and economical printing. Having produced these, they will work a selection up for presentation at the next meeting. At this meeting the designer will usually pave the way by outlining the original brief, restating the requirements and then explaining the creative thought processes involved in their solution. A range of cover designs and a variety of double-page spreads involving type and images will be shown to give the photographer a feel for the form, proportion and style of the book. There will be some indication of the grid structure, showing how the continuity will be held. A rough pagination may be provided in miniature, giving an indication of its flow through the entire content of the book.

The photographer should have a mental checklist from which the following questions could be asked of the designer and the design at this meeting:

- Does the proposed solution answer the brief?
- Is it an interesting and creative solution?
- Is it suitable for the market it is aimed at?
- Is the format ideal?
- Does it fulfil budget requirements?
- Has the designer missed anything out?

If the designs are not in keeping with the brief, the photographer is fully within their right to ask for more designs to be produced at no extra charge. However, if the initial design roughs are approved, then the designer will move on to developing the concept and refining it. Usually a full size dummy of the book is made with photocopies of the photographs and simulated text designating type areas. Headings will probably be hand lettered out or set on Apple Mac and all the elements will be carefully pulled together. Having calculated the available space for type, it is at this point that the typed manuscript is marked up. 'Mark up' is the process by which the designer gives instructions regarding typefaces and their point-sizes to the typesetter, who will then output it as bromide galleys or laser proofs.

In providing the manuscript to the designer, it should be typed wherever possible on the same machine to a consistent line length of around 60 to 65 characters, ranged left, ragged right. It should be typed in upper and lower case with any emphasis the author wants added only in pencil. The designer will mark up everything clearly and consistently. The cleaner the copy the quicker the typesetting can be processed and therefore the less expensive it will be. It is also useful if it can be double line spaced, to leave room for the designer's marks.

If the manuscript is to be provided on disc from a word processing package, it is very helpful to the typesetter if it is downloaded as an ASCII file. This provides only the bare bones of the text without all of its own software coding and therefore is more quickly formatted on the typesetter's system. What returns from them is dependent on whether the designer marked up the typesetting as individual pages or galleys. It will be photocopied by the designer and sent with the original manuscript to the photographer or the author for proof reading. At the same time as it is being proof read, the designer will assemble a set of the photocopies into the mocked up book, replacing the simulated text and checking everything fits as calculated. It should then resemble very closely the finished item.

It is important that the first proofing stage is completed carefully and that more than one person reads and checks the typesetting for mistakes. Any rewriting should be added at this stage before it goes back to the setters for updating. Any further necessary changes are made at this stage and re-presented to the photographer for further proofing and approval.

Once the designer has progressed through these first two stages of production, they can begin to assemble the camera ready artwork required for the printer. Generally the artwork will be completed in

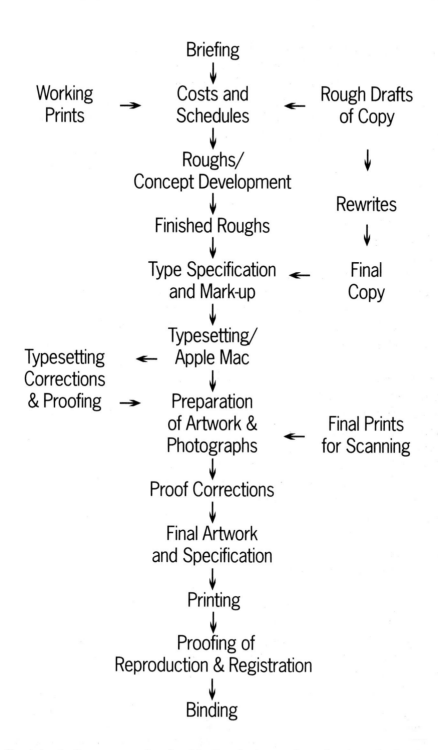

Briefing
↓

Working Prints → Costs and Schedules ← Rough Drafts of Copy
↓

Roughs/ Concept Development
↓   Rewrites

Finished Roughs
↓   ↓

Type Specification and Mark-up ← Final Copy
↓

Typesetting Corrections & Proofing ← Typesetting/ Apple Mac
↓

Typesetting Corrections & Proofing → Preparation of Artwork & Photographs ← Final Prints for Scanning
↓

Proof Corrections
↓

Final Artwork and Specification
↓

Printing
↓

Proofing of Reproduction & Registration
↓

Binding

flow chart of processes involved in the design and production of a book

double-page spreads on artboard or as pages output directly from the setter. The titles, headings, type and keylines for photographs will be put in position using the grid as a guide. All the photographs should now be in the designer's possession, as they will need to be sized and specified for the printer. Once the artwork has been completed and all overlays added, instructions regarding platemaking, screen and ink specifications are written neatly on a final overlay of layout or tracing paper, which also protects the art-work. Accompanying the artwork a general specification sheet should be typed, informing the printer of the nature of the job, the print run, the paper stock to be used and any finishing and binding requirements.

Either the artwork itself or photocopies of it, must be checked by the photographer and authors at this final stage. It is best to go through another checklist as you are looking at the artwork:

- Is the artwork pasted up in the correct order?
- Has the text all been corrected and given a final proof?
- Have all the photographs been correctly sized and positioned?
- Is the general specification letter correct?

Once the artwork has been checked thoroughly, the designer will require written clearance that it can go to the printer. This is usually called 'signing off' the artwork.

All the designer's processes of idea development, artwork and specification are now finished, but their involvement does not necessarily end here. The artwork may be handed over to the photographer to handle the print, or more commonly it goes to the publisher to be dealt with or the designer can take it through to completion themself. During the post-artwork production it is advisable to seek the assistance of an experienced print handler in order to deal with any problems that may occur and to correctly interpret the proof sheets of the book. The printing process is quite different to that of the photographic darkroom

Even if the designer does not handle the printing and therefore is not responsible for the final stage, they will be keen to see the book be printed to the highest standard and so generally will be happy to check ozalids, scatterproofs and chromalins that might be provided. Areas to check should include:

- All the process instructions have been carried out

- Tints are the correct percentages and are correctly laid
- Line and type reproduction is sharp and is neither over-exposed or too thinly exposed
- There are no unwanted keylines
- All the four colour photographs or halftones are clean and crisp
- No pictures have been accidentally flipped

On clearing the proofs or seeing new proofs of remade plates, the entire job will be run, any special finishes added and then the printed paper will be sent to the bindery for completion.

Alan Ward

using desktop publishing

Over recent years a number of designers have begun to explore and utilise computer-based design solutions revolving primarily around the use of Apple Macs. There are a number of typographers who have been able to take advantage of this technology to extend the range of services that they are to offer to their clients. Many of them are able to offer a design service which is particularly appropriate to bookwork.

One of the key advantages of the Mac is the flexibility that it can offer particularly in regard to typesetting and layout. Page layouts can be prepared quickly and can be amended easily. Its strength is also the ease with which page proofs can be produced presenting you with an exact visual of how they will appear.

Despite their apparent simplicity and user friendliness Macs do not convert the visually illiterate into top rank designers. There is as much poor quality work produced on Macs as there is good. However, an accomplished designer coupled with a Mac-based system is a marvellous combination for a publisher offering as it does savings of both time and money.

Laser proofs from a Mac can be used as camera ready artwork BUT their quality is far inferior to that produced by outputting to bromide or film through an imagesetter and I would therefore never recommend it unless a low-cost text-based publication is envisaged. Most lasers currently available offer 300dpi (dots per inch) quality compared to imagesetter quality of around 3000dpi. Over the next few years however it is likely that this will change as increasing technological development offers improved low-cost outputting systems.

This book, like most Cornerhouse titles since 1991, has been originated on a Mac-based system. More recently this facility has been brought in-house and a comprehensive production service subsequently made available to other book and magazine publishers.

The range of other developments focussing on Mac technology is frightening in its complexity and must be particularly worrying for traditionally based typesetters and also for repro houses. Direct colour proofing systems are now available and it is possible with relatively low-cost equipment to go from screen to finished film all through the Mac. It may even not be that long before it is possible to take this right through to the finished printed item. If you couple this with the development of electronic publishing systems then you begin to realise the fascinating potential proffered through the use of new technology. I have no doubt that if I am writing a revised edition of this book in five years time then much of my focus will be on new approaches to and new forms of publication.

understanding print

the printing process

It is not my intention to focus in any great detail on the printing processes, there are many excellent books that do this more than adequately. For me it is a bit like understanding cars. I tend to feel that whilst I need to know the basic principles I am more interested in what they can do than how they work.

Almost every book will be printed using the offset process. This is based on the principle that oil and water do not mix. When the printing plates are made the chemical process involved renders the areas to be printed receptive to the inks which are oil based whilst repelling moisture. The reverse is true for those areas that are to remain as un-printed. Originally water was used to repel the ink from the non-printing area though alcohol based fluids are now more generally used.

The printing plate is attached to a cylinder and ink is spread on to the image areas by a series of ink rollers which are adjustable to vary the flow of ink. These rollers are fed by ink ducts which are controlled electronically. With most presses a VDU will be used to indicate the ink levels being fed to each area of the plate. This introduction of electronic measurement means both that more precise control can be exerted and that a permanent record can be kept of the ink levels used on any printing job. This is particularly useful when it comes to setting up the press for a reprint.

The actual printing is not done directly from the plate. The ink is transferred from the plate to a blanket made of a soft rubber which is attached to another cylinder. It is this that imparts the image onto the sheet of paper. The image on the plate starts out as right reading (ie it is as you expect to see the final printed image). It is then reversed on to the blanket and then reversed back again when it prints on the paper. This is the principle known as offset.

For each colour used in the printing process a separate plate is needed and consequently a separate set of ink rollers and cylinders. Four or five colour presses are therefore not surprisingly very large pieces of equipment.

It always seems a miracle to me that the different cylinders, carrying the plates and blankets etc, manage to revolve so precisely, even at great speed, so that the four colour plates can reproduce an image in perfect registration. My unmechanical brain finds this precision incomprehensible. Again it's just like the car – how on earth do those four wheels turn in unison, or do they?

Most quality work is done on sheet-fed offset. This is where single sheets of paper are used. Web offset is used for the longer print runs and uses paper on a roll. This is the process used by the newspaper printers and for the larger circulation periodicals. While some excellent quality work can be achieved on Web it is generally recognised to be inferior to sheet-fed.

working with a printer

A printer can be either your worst enemy or your best friend. You have it in your total control to determine which of these it will be. From the outset you must do your utmost to ensure that the basis for your relationship is clearly set out and that there are few if any areas for future misunderstanding and disagreement. If you are clear about your objectives and your requirements and you explain them fully to your printer then you have a basis for working. If you do not, then expect things to go wrong. Precision and clarity are the keys.

- Always ensure that when you ask for an estimate you are as specific as you can possibly be.

- Always ensure that any changes to the specification are notified in writing and that you receive written confirmation from the printer of any price variation that will result. It is too easy to think that you have agreed one thing (usually that there will be no extra charge) and then two months later receive an additional charge that you were not expecting.

- Always check at every stage. If you are not happy with the results being achieved say so at the time not when you receive the finished books.

- If there is something you don't understand ask and ask immediately.

choosing a printer

There is no foolproof way of finding the right printer for your job. I always suggest that people start by looking at other books and catalogues. You will generally find the name of the printer of a book on the same page as the copyright details. Wherever possible talk to other people who have worked with particular printers – find out their experiences. Many galleries frequently produce highly illustrated catalogues, posters etc – ask for their views BUT always judge for yourself.

When you have a shortlist of appropriate printers ask to see some samples of their work. Tell them the type of project that you are working on and see if they have produced anything recently that you could see as an example. Many printers, particularly the larger ones and those specialising in the high quality colour printing needed for illustrated books, will have a sales rep who will be more than willing to come and see you to discuss the project. They will do their best to make you feel comfortable with them and you may be persuaded by their likeability. Remember though that these are the salesmen. Once you have placed the job with the company you may never see them again.

With this in mind I would always suggest that for any major book project you ask to go to the factory so that you will be able to meet the people who will deal with the production of your job. It is time consuming but it is best to clear any possible doubts now rather than when the machines are running. It is also true that if you can't strike up a rapport now before production starts then you have little chance later when any problems begin to arise. Look first for evidence of their expertise then look for interest and enthusiasm but more than anything look for someone who listens.

what is the process of working with a printer?

As soon as we have decided that we are interested in doing a book we approach at least three or four printers to ask for a provisional estimate to allow us to gauge the viability of the project. This may be as far as a year or more before the intended publication date. Usually there are still some unknown quantities but as far as we can we specify the following.

- Page size

  It is a very complex task trying to assess the most effective page size for a book. It sounds easy but it never is. You must recognise that you are limited by the sheet sizes of paper which are available and of course by the capacity of the press. As a general rule for cost-effectiveness you should ensure that on an A2 press you can get four pages to each side of the sheet (this is known as four to view) and on an A1 press eight pages (eight to view). Some examples of maximum page sizes and how to calculate them are included in the reference section.

  Bear in mind that if you were able to get twelve pages rather than eight pages from one side of paper then you would use 50% less paper. You would also use 50% fewer plates and require less printing time. Judicious sizing of the page can clearly be a very effective way of controlling cost.

- Number of pages

  Always aim to work in multiples of the number of pages that you are getting to a sheet of paper. In the case of eight to view you would get sixteen pages to a sheet. In the interests of cost you would therefore be best advised working in multiples of sixteen on an A1 press or eight on an A2 press.

  The minimum number of pages in a book that can be sewn as a separate section is eight. A four page section can not be properly sewn though it can be used to wrap around another section.

- Type of binding – case-bound or limp?

  When you are deciding what sort of binding to go for always think about two things. The market that is aimed for and the final retail price that you will be able to charge. A hardback, or case-binding should add a minimum of five or six pounds to the retail price that you would charge. If this is not feasible then you will be reducing the percentage profit available to you on the book. That may be a consequence that you are willing to accept but be aware of it before you make the commitment to hardback rather than after.

It used to be argued that softbacks did not get the consideration that they deserved – that libraries wouldn't buy and reviewers wouldn't review. We have had little evidence of this. It is certainly true that hardbacks are far more tactile and satisfying. They do feel rather more of an achievement BUT their extra cost is a very real disincentive to the book-buying public. We have found that even with titles where we have consciously kept to a very small price differential between the hardback and the softback editions the softback has outsold by a factor of three or four.

There are occasions when hardback makes absolute sense. If you are proposing a slim volume then case-binding can appear to add considerable substance and can increase the price that you will be able to charge quite dramatically. Equally if you are proposing a very small print run then the very fact of case-binding can be used as a positive factor in creating the sense of it being a limited edition.

- The expected number of colour images and black and white images and their anticipated placing

  This is our preliminary view of where the images will appear. For example will all the colour photographs be grouped together or will they be spread throughout the book so that every page has to be printed as four-colour work?

- A rough estimate of image sizes

  You may not be able to be exact but you will be able to gauge how many full or half page images you are going to use and you can make an estimate of their printed size. If all you say is that there will be 80 images in the book the printer will assume that each one will take the best part of a full page and they will price accordingly. They may of course be double page spreads in which case the printer will have underpriced that part of the job. It is more likely though that some of the images will occupy no more than 50% of the page area or even be small illustrations within the introductory text. In that case the quotation would be considerably overpriced.

- How do we want black and white photographs reproduced?

Will they be printed as single black (monochrome), or duotone, or will we use four colour process? If you are including black and white and colour photographs together in a book it can be very expensive to use duotone and colour on the same side of the printed sheet. This is because you would be using four colours for the colour images plus an extra black for the second black in the duotone. If the press is a four colour press then you would immediately need to be running each sheet through twice. Four colour process does work quite well however in giving the images a good tonal range. The black and white photographs in our book "Looking for Love" are reproduced in this way.

- Will a varnish be added?

Adding a machine varnish to the image area helps to bring out the gloss in the image and improves the sense of depth. An additional set of printing plates is required and there are therefore cost implications. I would usually ask for machine varnish to be quoted as a separate option. A varnish can be added either on-line, meaning that it is applied at the same time as the printing is done, or off-line, meaning that it is done at a later stage by putting the printed sheets through the press again. On-line is cheaper but does not give as high a gloss finish.

- The weight and type of the paper

If the book we are producing is primarily images rather than text then we will use 170 gsm as a general rule. If it is more than 150 pages then we may consider dropping the paper weight to 150 gsm. We would only use lighter weight paper for a text based book.

We tend to go for a matt coated paper rather than a gloss paper (known as an art paper). This is a personal preference. Coated papers are to my mind the best at reproducing photographs. They allow better definition and closer facsimile colour reproduction. They also have the advantage that they are more opaque which means that they can also hold stronger ink densities with less show through of what is printed on the other side.

The cost of paper is always a significant element in any printing job particularly if you are using the better quality and therefore more expensive materials. Different papers have different characteristics and can alter the effect of a printed photograph quite dramatically. A specialist printer will have a range of papers that they prefer and with which they have had considerable experience. A printer will generally ensure that they can suggest a range of materials to cover all budgets. Unless you are specifying a top of the range paper I take the view that you are better to ask the printer to suggest their favoured material and to ask for samples of any recent jobs that they have printed on it.

The paper manufacturers and paper merchants are very good at supplying sample swatches. They also produce printed samples to show how their papers respond to various printing techniques. These are helpful but I would still have to say that the best sample to base any decision on is the one that has been printed by one of the printers that you have short-listed for your job.

• Quantity

At this stage we will probably have very little idea of the quantity that we are going to produce, however, we will know that it will be 2,000 plus. (It is almost impossible to achieve viability with a lower print run unless there is substantial outside funding). We will therefore ask that the quote be based on 2,000 copies and for a run on price per 500 or 1000 copies. This then allows us to have a rough estimate of the costs for a much larger print run.

When looking at quantity always try to be realistic in your assess-ment of the likely number of sales that you can achieve. It is far less disheartening to have to go for a reprint after six months than to still have unsold copies after six years. Do not be deceived into only thinking about unit cost.

We ask for estimates in a standard way using the form that is reproduced on the next page.

CORNERHOUSE PUBLICATIONS

70 Oxford Street • Manchester • M1 5NH   tel 061 228 7621 • fax 061 236 7323

ESTIMATE REQUEST

Title: ....   **Production Period:** ....

Repro: Supplied as CRC/Page Film   Image scans supplied

Prints: .... colour   .... black & white for mono/duotone

Transparencies: .... colour   .... black & white for mono/duotone

Image sizes: ....

          ....   **Price**

Proofs: Ozalids   ....

          Chromalins   full set/scatter proofs   ....

          Machine Proofs   full set/scatter proofs   ....

          scanning   ....

          film assembly   ....

          Reduction for page film supplied   ....

Printing: Extent ....   Page size ....   Portrait/Landscape

Body: .... pps printed .... pps printed ....

          .... pps printed .... pps printed ....   **Price to Book blocks**   ....

Ends: .... pps printed ....

Cover: .... pps printed ....

Jacket: .... pps printed ....

Paper: Body   ....   gsm   ....

          Ends   ....   gsm   ....

          Cover   ....   gsm   ....   **Paper Cost**   ....

Alternative paper: Body   ....   gsm   ....

          Ends   ....   gsm   ....

          Cover   ....   gsm   ....   **Paper Cost**   ....

Finishing:

Softback: Section sewn, Covers drawn on Cover Laminated Gloss/Matt

Hardback: Cased in, blocking on spine/on front and spine/End Papers/Jackette

Quantity:

Softback: .... copies   Hardback: .... copies
          plus 500/1000 copies run-on   plus 500/1000 copies run on

Delivery: To one UK address

C
CORNERHOUSE
PUBLICATIONS

Once we have received the estimates for the job we will begin to look at the viability of the project. How does the production cost compare to what we believe to be the realistic retail price for the book? Printers' estimates vary considerably in the way that they are presented. Some will give a grand total with very little detail, others will separate out each item and allocate a detailed cost. Pages 58 and 59 show the quotation offered to us by Balding and Mansell for our recent publication "Broken Images" by David Parker.

We are now in a position to be able to develop a preliminary budget for the project, and we will also have the information that will allow us to begin approaching any of the funding bodies for grant-aid support, or to make approaches to other publishers to see if they might be interested in a co-production.

If all the figures add up then we may have a project with which we can proceed.

It is then back to pre-production – completing the editing, sequencing, preliminary design work and, if there is a need for it, producing the dummy.

The next step for me is to produce a page order so that I can get a very clear view of the implications that our editorial decisions are likely to have on the cost of the project. Essentially this is a matter of listing each page and indicating what is intended to go on it. I use a computer and a standard spreadsheet programme to help me with this, mainly because it allows me to make any necessary revisions very quickly. There is no reason why you can't do this just using pen and paper. Pages 60 and 61 show the running order for the Bruce Gilden book "Facing New York", as an example of the sort of print-out I get.

Balding + Mansell plc

Park Works, 103 Norwich Road, Wisbech, Cambs PE13 2AX

Telephone 0945 582011 Telex 32162 Fax 0945 63228 or 63910

Cornerhouse Publications
70 Oxford Street
Manchester
M1 5NH

Attention: Dewi Lewis

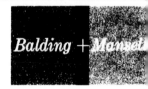

24th June 1992

"BROKEN IMAGES"   *Estimate*   998

SPECIFICATION

Quantity:	2,500 copies in all as 2,000 limp and 500 cased and per 500 run on limp and cased. NB - Cased run on from limp.

Size:	240 x 300mm landscape
4 x 6pp:	240 x 885mm (300 + 295 + 290) throwout falling short
Jacket:	246 x 888mm maximum outspread of foredge

Printing:

Body
96 pages printed offset in 4 process colours as 72 pages
(9 x 8pp sections) plus 24 pages (4 x 6pp sections which
wrap 4 of the 8pp sections).

Cover
4 pages printed offset in 4 process colours plus OPP
Gloss lamination one side only. Inner not printed.

Jacket
Printed offset in 4 process colours and OPP Gloss
laminated one side only.

Endpapers
2 x 4pp (cased only) not printed.

Finishing:
Fold, 9 x 8pp and 4 x 6pp sections, wrap 6pp round 8pp.
Gather, collate and thread sew and -
a) Cover drawn into square backs, trimmed flush 3 edges.
Packed in binders cartons.
b) 2 x 4pp tinted endpapers tipped on, edges cut. Square
back, lined, head and tial bands affixed. Full bound
in linson cloth over 3mm greyboard with board hollow.
Foil blocked on spine in one colour. Jacketed and
packed binders cartons.

Material:	Body:	Chromomat 170gsm
	Cover:	Chromomat 300gsm
	Jacket:	Comet Art 135gsm
	Endpapers:	Colorplan Plain 135gsm

Balding + Mansell plc Registered office 103 Norwich Road, Wisbech, England. Registered number 2479728

Reproduction:

200 line screen
24 colour transparencies and complete page camera ready
line artwork to be supplied to us for reproduction as:
33 to 195 x 248mm
21 to 110 x 140mm
 2 to 110 x 248mm
 4 to 195 x 464mm
11 to 49 x 62mm
 3 to 75 x 95mm squared up colour halftones.
All squared camera ready artwork to same size in one
colour (line only). No tint laying allowed for.

Composition:

Nil. Complete page camera ready artwork to be supplied
to us.

Proofs:

Assembled ozalids of body - 2 copies
Matchprint proof of cover and jacket - 1 copy of each
See also below

Delivery:

In bulk to one address within 100 mile radius of Wisbech.

Prices:

To planned foils, body, cover, jacket   £4,999

Extra:

Full set of in-track Matchprints 1 copy   £1,247

Extra:

Full set 1-sided, wet, in-track proofs
12 copies   £4,218

Extra:

To random assemble 10 4-colour pictures
and provide 1 Matchprint proof   £ 259

		2,500 copies in all	500 run on limp	500 run on cased
Plates and printing -	Body	£ 4,148	£ 178	£ 178
	Cover	£ 307	£ 9	--
	Jacket	£ 284	--	£ 21
Materials -	Body	£ 2,158	£ 360	£ 360
	Cover	£ 234	£ 39	--
	Jacket	£ 69	--	£ 34
	Endpapers	£ 131	--	£ 67
Finishing -	To sewn book blocks	£ 1,084	£ 186	£ 186
	Limp binding	£ 230	£ 40	--
	Cased binding	£ 1,391	--	£ 943
Lamination -	Cover	£ 110	£ 27	--
	Jacket	£ 57	--	£ 57
Delivery		£ 113	£ 5	£ 5
	Total	£10,316	£ 844	£1,851

Extra:

For individual shrink wrapping   £65 per 500

Page Layout   Facing New York by Bruce Gilden

Page Size   248mm x 338mm

Section	Print	Page	Contents	Image size
Jacket	Duotone + 2 Colours Front Cover			
Section 1 printed 1/0	SELF END	1	SELF END	
	Black only	2	Line illustration	
	Black only	3	Line illustration	
		4	BLANK	
Section 2 Duotone one side	Duo	1	Pic 1	228 x 338
		2	Dedication	
	Black only	3	Half-Title	
	Duo	4	Pic 2	470 x 316
	Duo	5	Pic 2	Double Page
		6	BLANK	
		7	TEXT	
		8	BLANK	
Section 3 Duotone Both sides		9	Pic 3	228 x 338
		10	Pic 4	470 x316
		11	Pic 4	Double Page
		12	BLANK	
		13	Pic 5	228 x 338
		14	Pic 6	470 x316
		15	Pic 6	Double Page
Section 4 Duotone Both sides		17	Pic 7	Double Page
		18	BLANK	
		19	Pic 8	228 x 338
		20	BLANK	
		21	Pic 9	228 x 338
		22	Pic 10	470 x 316
		23	Pic 10	Double Page
		24	BLANK	
Section 5 Duotone Both sides		25	Pic 11	228 x 338
		26	Pic 12	470 x 316
		27	Pic 12	Double Page
		28	BLANK	
		29	Pic 13	228 x 338
		30	Pic 14	470 x 316
		31	Pic 14	Double Page
		32	BLANK	
Section 6 Duotone Both sides		33	Pic 15	228 x 338
		34	Pic 16	470 x 316
		35	Pic 16	Double Page
		36	Pic 17	470 x 316
		37	Pic 17	Double Page
		38	BLANK	
		39	Pic 18	228 x 338
		40	Pic 19	470 x 316
Section 7 Duotone Both sides		41	Pic 19	Double Page
		42	BLANK	
		43	Pic 20	228 x 338

Section 7 (contd)		44	BLANK	
		45	Pic 21	228 x 338
		46	Pic 22	470 x 316
		47	Pic 22	Double Page
		48	BLANK	
Section 8		49	Pic 23	228 x 338
Duotone		50	Pic 24	470 x 316
Both sides		51	Pic 24	Double Page
		52	Pic 25	470 x 316
		53	Pic 25	Double Page
		54	BLANK	
		55	Pic 26	228 x 338
		56	BLANK	
Section 9		57	Pic 27	228 x 338
Duotone		58	BLANK	
Both sides		59	Pic 28	228 x 338
		60	Pic 29	470 x 316
		61	Pic 29	Double Page
		62	BLANK	
		63	Pic 30	228 x 338
		64	BLANK	
Section 10		65	Pic 31	228 x 338
Duotone		66	Pic 32	470 x 316
Both sides		67	Pic 32	Double Page
		68	BLANK	
		69	Pic 33	228 x 338
		70	Pic 34	470 x 316
		71	Pic 34	Double Page
		72	BLANK	
Section 11		73	Pic 35	228 x 338
Duotone		74	BLANK	
Both sides		75	Pic 36	228 x 338
		76	Pic 37	470 x 316
		77	Pic 37	Double Page
		78	BLANK	
		79	Pic 38	228 x 338
		80	BLANK	
Section 12		81	Pic 39	228 x 338
Duotone		82	Pic 40	470 x 316
Both sides		83	Pic 40	Double Page
		84	BLANK	
		85	Pic 41	228 x 338
		86	Pic 42	470 x 316
		87	Pic 42	Double Page
		88	BLANK	
Section 13		89	Pic 43	228 x 338
Duotone		90	Pic 44	470 x 316
Both sides		91	Pic 44	Double Page
		92	Blank	
Section 14		1	Blank	
printed 1/0	Black only	2	Line illustration	
	Black only	3	Line illustration	
	SELF END	4	SELF END	

From this example I can work out where I need to be printing in duotone and where I can use single colour black.

Print 1/1 means that it will be one colour on each side of the sheet of paper.

Print 2/1 means duotone on one side and single black on the other.

Print 4/0 would mean four colour process on one side and nothing on the other.

An alternative to my spreadsheet approach is to use a flat plan. This tends to be favoured by designers. Each double page spread is drawn out as two small boxes with contents details marked on them. The diagram opposite illustrates this.

By using these approaches I can see at a glance any easy way in which I might be able to save some money. It might be, for example, that by including one blank page I can avoid having to print as four colour process one side of a sheet of paper. A small rearrangement such as this can save a few hundred pounds.

Now that I have my running order I can move on to making decisions about the sizing of the images I have allowed for.

delivering the finished artwork

Deadlines come very quickly and it is rare not be under some pressure as the printer's deadline approaches. As a result it is very tempting to suggest to the printer that you send the job across to them in bits – images first, text to follow a few days later and then perhaps the jacket artwork at the beginning of the following week. Never ever get yourself in this position. Always ensure that you send the complete book or you are opening yourself up to misunderstandings and mis-interpretations which may end up not only with the book being rather different to how you had intended but also additional charges being levied. It is very easy for mistakes to be made at artwork stage – an inconsistency here or there – and these will not be picked up by you or by the repro house unless they are doing the job as one item.

A simple example would be when you ask for a set of images to be

Page Plan **Title:** _____

Page Size   156mm x 234mm

Images   Black & White ☐   Duotone ▨   Four-Colour ■

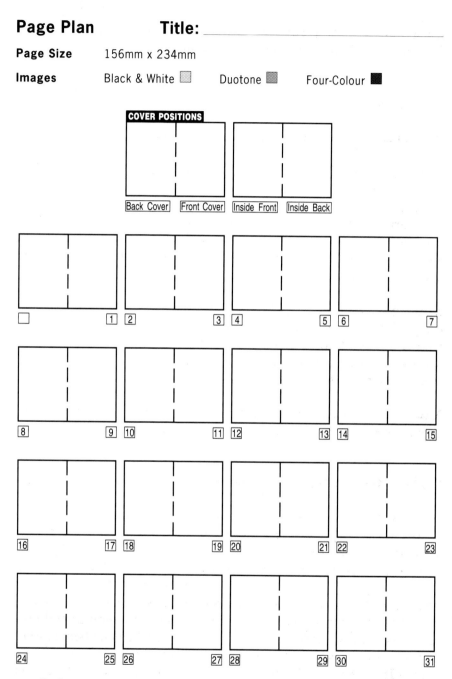

Initially the projected contents of each page should be added in pencil. When, several rubbers later, the layout is finalised, images and text can be colour-coded so that the basic layout of the book has a clear visual representation. Apart from the covers, the 8-page sections illustrated above do not correspond with printer's sections.

scanned to a particular size and then a few days later you send the artwork for the pages on which the images are to be placed. Sod's Law says that the scanning sizes for at least some of the images are bound to be wrong and so either you must amend the artwork or rescan the appropriate images.

I am often asked what size and type of photographic print should be provided for the printer to work from. It depends very much on the type of book and to a lesser extent on the type of images. However, there are some basic ground-rules.

- Prints should always be at least the same size as they are to be printed. It is always preferable to reduce rather than enlarge.

- They should all be printed on the same paper with a similar balance and tone.

- The printing should be to the best possible quality achievable.

- Always check with the printer to see the maximum size prints that the repro house can handle.

- As a general guide we would normally consider 16" x 12" (or the equivalent in other formats) as a good size with which to work.

If you work with transparencies then there are some problems. Transparencies are excellent for scanning and do produce very good results. Because of their size, however, they are very difficult to use at proofing stage, particularly when you are on press and trying to compare back to the original. With a print you can lay it against the printed image to make a direct comparison whereas with a transparency you have to rely more instinctively on your sense of colour.

Another problem is that with transparencies you are using the original and however carefully it is treated by the repro house and the printer there remains a risk of damage. You should therefore always ensure that whilst you work with the originals you also have high quality duplicates as backup in case of damage.

Prints can also be damaged and therefore it is again important that you check that you have the negative before you hand over what could be the one and only print.

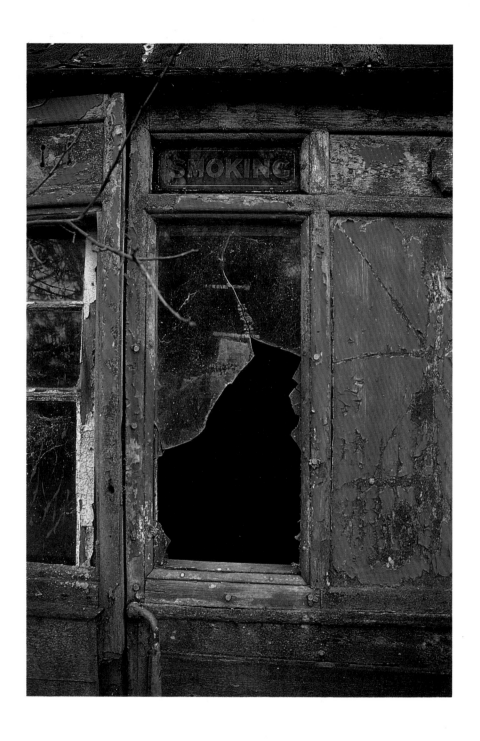

Four-colour process plus varnish

Black and white photograph
C.L.R. James by Steve Pyke
from the forthcoming book *The Philosophers*

Colour photograph
by Dave Thomas
from the forthcoming book *Ramshackles*

This section of photographs was printed by Jackson Wilson, Unit 4, Gelderd Trading Estate, West Vale, Leeds LS12 6BD

Alan Ward outlined earlier the checks that he advises before sending off artwork. I make no apology for repeating many of them at this point. Always make sure of the following:

- That every image is clearly identified both with a number and with the size to which it is to be printed. It is very helpful for the repro house for this to be marked on the front. Given that we are usually dealing with exhibition prints we avoid damage by attaching either a post-it note or a sheet of paper carefully clipped to the front. If any image could be mistakenly read upside down or on its side then mark it clearly showing top and bottom.

- That the placing of each image is clearly marked on the artwork.

- That there is a note explaining anything that might be misunderstood. If it can be it probably will.

- Provide a check list of everything that is included in the package.

- Include a reconfirmation of everything that has been agreed with the printer. The type of proofs required, page size, type of paper, images to be varnished or not, quantity etc.

- Remember that when you hand over the artwork the editorial phase of book production has finished. All decisions should have been taken and changes will be not only extremely expensive but will also undermine the future working relationship with the printer.

Once you have sent off the work don't disappear for a three week holiday – you may be needed. Again Sod's Law says that when you're not there you'll be wanted.

repro

Many printers will subcontract parts of the production process for a book. Repro is frequently handled in this way. Repro is the conversion of the artwork that you have provided into film ready for making the plates that will be used on the press. When the printer receives your artwork and images they will first check that the job matches the initial specification and that the instructions that you or the designer have given can be understood. They will then pass the work across for repro. There are two main elements; firstly the camera work or the scanning and secondly the film assembly.

Scanning is now generally favoured in preference to using a camera. It is excellent at producing fine detail within the image and can also be very effective in image manipulation adding characteristics of contrast or colour saturation which were not present in the original.

Once all the photographs to be used in a book have been scanned they are assembled with the film that has been produced from the base artwork to create a page film. This is known as dropping in an image. Individual pages are then assembled in the sequence necessary for the printing plate. Film assembly requires great accuracy particularly in the case of colour or duotone work where the registration between the different colour films must be absolutely perfect.

imposition

When the individual pages are placed together in the order necessary for platemaking this is known as the imposition. This is a confusing concept to get to grips with initially mainly because when you look at the sequence of pages on a printed sheet it always looks as if the sequence is totally wrong. What you have to remember is that after the sheet of paper has been printed it is then folded and it is at this point that the sequence must work, not when you look at the single sheet.

When you are proofing anything for a printer always make it clear that you have not checked the imposition and that this is their responsibility. Once you get into printed sheets with more than eight pages printed on one side (known as eight to view) it becomes very difficult to check whether or not the imposition is correct.

proofing

The next stage in the process is receiving proofs. Essentially there are three types:

- Non-printed proofs

  This would include chromalins and match proofs. These are both proofing processes that seek to replicate the final printed image. Because they do not use the same process as printing I never believe that they can be fully relied on. They do, however, give a very good guide. They will show any colour cast that has been added at repro stage and they will also indicate the strength of the colour in the image – dense blacks, rich reds etc. These proofs are generally only prepared for the images in the book and not for the page layouts. For these you will need ozalids.

The difficulty I have always found is that of knowing why a colour proof is wrong when it clearly is. It is not an easy task to judge which of the process colours is changing the balance of an image. I will therefore always talk through with the printer or with repro any proofs that seem to be a problem.

- Machine proofs

Machine proofs are generally far more expensive. They are not necessarily better. Much machine proofing is done in-house at repro and not by the printer. As a result they are not using the press on which the job will finally be printed and consequently the results may be rather different. The ideal is to arrange for machine proofs to be done by the printer that you have selected on the press that they will use. In this way you will have removed as many of the variables as you possibly can.

Despite their cost machine proofs can be very cost effective if you want to produce advance sheets for making up as sales blads to begin the process of generating interest and sales in a book. This is particularly true with jackets and there is therefore a logic in going to machine proofs for the jacket.

- Ozalids

Also known as blues, ozalids are cheap proofs of the full book. They are produced by a dye-line process and look rather similar to architects blueprints. They are taken from assembled film prior to platemaking. They can not be used to gauge quality but they are very important for checking accuracy and ensuring that no mistakes have crept in at the repro stage. I always ask for the ozalids to be provided as f & gs. This means that they are presented to me folded and guillotined in page sequence so that I can check them easily. In this way they will read just like the finished book.

Once the proofs are ready they will be sent out to you with the original artwork and the images. Generally you will receive the image proofs first and then once these have been agreed ozalids will be made up and sent out. Spending time to check them thoroughly is absolutely essential. The process of checking should be as methodical as possible. I have noticed that many photographers take considerable pains to check that the image reproduction is acceptable whilst never checking (through the ozalids) to see whether the sequence is correct. I work in the following way:

Checking to colour

- Work in a well-lit, daylight area where the quality of light is even. Chromalins are produced for viewing in colour corrected lighting conditions. This can prove difficult to achieve at home or at work but as long as the light is even you can effectively gauge the proofing quality.

- Compare each proof to the original image. Lay areas of colour next to each other to allow a more direct relationship to be achieved. Make a note on any image that you are not happy with or uncertain about, clip it to the proof and keep that with the original image. When you have finished this process of checking look again at any of the proof images with which you are unhappy. You will probably be able to discern a similar problem in all of them – for example a green colour cast – again make notes.

- Checking proofs should always be done as a continuous and complete exercise. If you do half now and half tomorrow your visual response may be different. It also needs to be done quickly – the printers can't do anything until you send back the work.

Checking ozalids

- Start by checking that the sequence of images is correct and that nothing has been reversed (known as flipping) or turned upside down.

- Check that every image is squared up properly and that the edge of each image area is clean and sharp. You may notice lines continuing along the edge of an image which occur during the film assembly stage. These must be removed.

- Read every word of text AND get someone else to reread the text for you. It is too easy to miss things, particularly when you have read a text for the nth time.

- Check every page number.

- Check every page for marks or blemishes. Circle every single mark clearly. Most of these will not be on the film but there may be some that are and that should be removed before platemaking.

Many printers will require you to sign off the proofs. This is your confirmation that what has been presented to you is acceptable and can therefore go to press. Clearly you should only sign off when you are happy with the work.

on the presses

There is no doubt that however good the printer is the best work can be achieved if you are on press for the job. There is a very delicate balance to be achieved if you want to get the best out of your printer. You need to create a partnership with the pressman, not a master-servant relationship. You should recognise that they have the experience and if you are trying to achieve a particular result they will almost certainly have the expertise to translate your ideas into reality. Ultimately you need them far more than they need you – so tread carefully, treat them as living, breathing, feeling, human beings.

There is one reality of which you should always be aware when on press and that is the reality that time is money. Time will have been allocated by the printer for making ready on each plate. This means the time it takes to clean down the machines, put on the next plate or plates and run trial sheets through until a satisfactory result has been achieved. If you take excessive time in agreeing each sheet there may be a financial penalty. Leave the pressman alone until he presents you with what he thinks is a printed sheet that can be run. At this point you will check it with him and if it is acceptable you will sign it off and the presses will roll. Check these sheets thoroughly. Look for the following:

- Any marks, blemishes or dust spots (known as hickeys) both on the images and on the white space. These can be removed from the plate relatively easily.

- Check for the colour match to the proof or to the original print. There may be a need to adjust the amount of one colour of ink being fed to the press.

- Check for the density of ink. Are the blacks solid enough? Always remember that when the ink is wet it will tend to give a much richer, glossier appearance than will be finally achieved. The inks will dry down and the image will flatten slightly. If you are adding varnish as a seperate operation then that will bring some of the gloss and depth back to the image.

- Discuss any of your concerns with the pressman. Know what you are looking for and tell him.

- When you are on press you must make your decisions quickly and firmly. This is not the time to vacillate.

- Always look at a printed sheet as a whole. Taking up a colour for one image may impact on another image on the sheet which you are perfectly happy with. Always ask the pressman what will happen with any variations that you want to try before you try them.

- DON'T forget that it is your book. They are your photographs. If you really are having major problems getting the results that you should, do not get pressured into agreeing the print until you are satisfied.

- DON'T make changes simply to see what will happen. I have seen photographers who were happy with the printed sheet ask for less black ink and then more just to see what the end results would be. This may be acceptable for the first sheet being printed in that it allows the photographer to see a sense of the potential, but it is no help to anyone when it is repeated on future sheets. It will also open you up to additional charges for the time spent in this process.

- ALWAYS REMEMBER that you are printing a book and therefore there must be a consistency of print quality and density throughout. The pressman will be attempting to achieve this balance. If you make significant adjustments between one sheet and another you will be undermining this.

Once you have agreed the sheet then the press will be switched on. Leave the pressman alone at this point – you have done your job. They will check the printed sheets at regular intervals against the agreed sheet to ensure that there are no variations creeping in.

Being on press is not one of the most exciting ways of spending your time. If you are lucky the machines will be running on twelve hour shifts – if you are unlucky twenty-four hour shifts. You will generally be needed every two to three hours depending on the length of the print run. The result is an awful lot of waiting around. Try to use this time as effectively as you can – find out more about printing, talk to the pressmen in their quieter moments, watch other jobs that are going through. Do remember though that people have a job of work to do and so try not to be too intrusive.

after press

The next stage is finishing. The printed sheets are folded and then guillotined to form the sections of the book, which are then stitched together before the covers are drawn on.

Once a book has been bound together you are at the point of no return. If there is a mistake in the book then it really is too late. You can add an erratum slip but not a lot more. With this in mind I have always added a checking process before the binding stage. I ask the printer to put together a copy of the complete book as folded and guillotined sections. This is just like looking at the book except it is unbound. It means that if there is a problem that I have not spotted previously then I can take a decision now about how serious it is and if necessary arrange a reprint of the problem pages.

This is a moment I hate. I really want to be enjoying the book but instead I am searching for the flaws, anxiously hoping that nothing has escaped my eye. Once I am happy that everything is alright then I give the go ahead for the binding and sit back relieved.

Receiving advance copies of a new book is a marvellous experience. It must be even more so for the photographer or for an author. After all the months or even years of picture-making or writing, planning and preparation to see the finished result is a great satisfaction. That satisfaction is however never absolute. As you get to know the book you will see things that could have been done differently, ideas that haven't quite worked the way that you imagined, and usually one typesetting error that you never quite understand how you missed.

Now your book is ready to face the world. You will probably feel that you have been working flat out on it forever. The truth is that you have scarcely begun. The real hard work comes in trying to get the book out into the world and on to the bookshop shelves.

marketing and publicity

Publishing is a very easy way to lose a lot of money very quickly. The production of a book is a complex process but in comparison to the act of selling and distribution it is like falling off the proverbial log. For all publishers, and perhaps more particularly for gallery publishers and self-publishers, it is just too easy to end up with unsold and apparently unsaleable stocks of books.

Short-run publications can rarely sustain more than the most modest of marketing and publicity budgets. Their profitability is so marginal that every pound of expenditure in this area can simply compound the loss. It is therefore absolutely critical that you take time analysing what you can and cannot afford to spend on marketing and publicity. Start by looking at what can be achieved for the price of a stamp and a simple leaflet before you think of investing your money in space advertising or in lavish print. Think about the profit that you will be making from every book sold and then compare that to the cost of the approach that you are considering.

Even if you are not self-publishing your book expect to take an active role in its marketing. You should be willing to give as much time as is needed in the first two months. Each effort you make at this stage will be significant in helping to generate adequate press and media interest. Make sure that you keep your publisher fully informed of anything which could help book sales – an exhibition, a magazine feature, any award or nomination for an award – all of these can be effectively exploited by a publicity-minded publisher.

For the self-publisher, however, the hard work will last for considerably longer than two months. Expect the next year to be committed almost exclusively to dealing with your book and you won't be far wrong.

advance information sheets

One of the first pieces of information that you should prepare is the AI (Advance Information) sheet.

AI sheets are dispatched well in advance of publication, at least three months and up to six months. The larger publishers will circulate their AI sheets even earlier.

They are sent to sales reps at home and abroad, to key bookshops, wholesalers and to publishers and others that you may wish to keep informed.

The information should be presented in a simple and easily readable manner and should be kept to one side of A4.

What to include:

- Title, subtitle, author.

- ISBN

- Page size and number of pages

- Number of photographs – colour or black and white

- Intended publication date and price

- Key Selling Points – reasons for the bookshops to stock it. What is new or special about it. This may link to the next point.

- Any promotional support – exhibitions, confirmed magazine portfolios or features, point of sale and display material etc.

- A brief description of the subject matter

- A brief list of contents – a book such as this one would have its key chapter headings listed. For a monograph you would combine description and content.

- Intended readership – don't make ludicrous claims. Try to assess reasonably objectively the range of people whose interests might link back to your title.

- Author details – this is not a time to be modest nor is it the time to call yourself Britain's best known landscape photographer unless it is true.

- Publishers name, address and telephone number.

This is obviously a lot of information to cover and it is therefore critical that you think very clearly about the way it is presented. An example of an AI sheet prepared for one of our titles is reproduced on page 82.

press releases

A press release should, like an AI sheet, be kept to one side of A4. It seems an obvious thing to say but it should be interesting (very many press releases are not and come across as an act of duty by the writer rather than an act of enthusiasm). You should bear in mind that some papers finding themselves with space and little time will be looking for fillers. If the release is written in such a way that is suitable they may well use a paragraph or two, or even the whole piece, almost verbatim. This is particularly true of the smaller regional papers. It is therefore important to ensure that you include all the relevant information to allow readers to place orders for your book through their local shop.

I tend to find that a single press release is insufficient and that generally you should expect to prepare three variations.

- One for the local or regional press. This would be aimed towards the local interest approach – local photographer, or subject matter relating to the region.

- One for the more specialist photographic press. This would perhaps seek to locate the photographer within current or historical photographic practice.

- One for the magazines, national newspapers and the national media. This is more likely to stress the subject matter.

There is nothing wrong in adding further variations but it is important that you keep a proper record of who has received what.

ADVANCED TITLE
INFORMATION

CORNERHOUSE
PUBLICATIONS

BROKEN IMAGES
The Nazca Lines

Photographs by David Parker
Introduction by Dr Helaine Silverman

Publication Date: **5 October 1992**

Price	**£13.95/softback** **£18.95/hardback**
Size	**96pp/240mm x 300mm**
Illustrations	**74 colour photographs**
ISBN	**0 948797 86 X** (softback) **0 948797 87 8** (hardback)

Key Selling Points
- Major subject of Photographic, Archaeological, and Geographic interest
- Comprehensive introduction by leading archaeologist Dr Helaine Silverman
- Touring exhibition based on the book
- Considerable media interest already

Summary

For 50 years Maria Reiche has held effective control over one of the most extra-ordinary archaeological sites in the world – Nazca, in Peru. The story of Nazca is one of great drama. It is the story of Reiche's commitment and obsession to control and protect the past, and of the collision between the underdeveloped and developed world; of global tourism and the disjunction of past and present, wealthy and poor.

Although the existence of lines on the Nazca pampa was known earlier this century it was not until 1952 that the first figure (a monkey) was discovered by Reiche. Immense in scale and visible only from the air, it was the first of a number of discoveries of bird and animal figures mysteriously drawn on the pampa that were to focus world attention on the area. For many, these figures in the landscape were seen as the work of extra-terrestrial beings; for others they were a route to tourist dollars and previously unknown wealth.

To coincide with the 40 years since Reiche made her discovery of the first figure, Cornerhouse is publishing **Broken Images** by David Parker, whose colour photographs vividly portray the compelling story of Nazca – the town, its people and their past. In an extensive introduction respected archaeologist Helene Silverman tells the story of Reiche and the Nazca lines, and the intellectual and physical power struggle of archaeologists to control this extraordinary landscape.

CORNERHOUSE PUBLICATIONS • 70 OXFORD STREET • MANCHESTER • M1 5NH
telephone 061 228 7621 • fax 061 236 7323

advanced information sheet

There will always be magazines and newspapers which you see as a priority for coverage. With these you should follow up the press release with a phone call. When you do this always be prepared. Have all the relevant information close to hand and also think about the ways in which you can enthuse the journalist with whom you will be speaking. They will be willing to consider any interesting angle that you might have. Never forget that you are fighting for space and attention with a mass of competing stories. Think of it from the journalist's point of view. What is it that might make it especially interesting to them? An example of a press release related to one of our titles is reproduced on page 84.

what else should you send?

Along with the press release you can send out other material

- Jackets or covers – it is always worth while when printing to arrange for additional, run-on copies. These are useful to send out as visual support material.

- Press photos – we send these out sparingly to those people whom we are fairly certain will use them (they are expensive and despite requests few get returned). We do, however, always make it clear that press prints are available on request.

- Sheets or images from the printed book – we will often send out sample pages when these are available. They will either be in the form of folded and guillotined sections from the book or early printed sheets trimmed down.

- Typescript copies of the accompanying text – for a few reviewers we will send out either an abridged version or the final version of any accompanying text to the book. This can be a help to those writers who are likely to give a more extensive review.

review copies

Putting together an effective review copy list is a very important and time-consuming task. For the photography publisher the distribution list is likely to cover international as well as UK magazines and

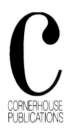

CORNERHOUSE
PUBLICATIONS

PRESS RELEASE

• **New Title** •

TO THE DOGS
by Elliot Erwitt

"I would get into trouble if I took pictures of people doing some of these things."

It's just possible that even Madonna would shy away from being snapped in some of the poses to be found in this month's other major new book ...

To the Dogs is devoted to Elliott Erwitt's long-time observation of the canine species and what it reveals about the human one. *"This book is not about dogs,"* he declares in his wryly entertaining introductory essay. *These are, in fact, not pictures of dogs at all. Look again."* Indeed, these endearing portraits of pooches reveal such an uncanny resemblance between hound and human that it is hard not to put words into their mouths and ideas into their heads.

Featuring dogs of almost every breed and description in their native settings around the world, this is a truly cosmopolitan canine collection.

Elliott Erwitt is a photojournalist and one of the earliest members of the illustrious Magnum Photo Agency. His work has been widely published and he has had one-man exhibitions throughout the world.

Published by D.A.P./SCALO
177 duotone plates • 144 pages hardback
ISBN 1 881616 01 0 • £25.00
Distributed in the UK by Cornerhouse

**For further information or press prints
please contact Alison Buchan**

Publisher Of The Year
SUNDAY TIMES
Small
1990

press release

CORNERHOUSE PUBLICATIONS • 70 OXFORD STREET • MANCHESTER • M1 5NH
telephone 061 228 7621 • fax 061 236 7323

reviewers. The first stage is to try and get to the know the key magazines in each of the countries that you wish to cover. Wherever possible get hold of copies of the magazines themselves to see the sort of review coverage that is given. Don't simply go for right-sounding magazines.

At the UK level check through magazines and newspapers. With the national press always find out who the individuals are who are most likely to give you coverage.

Sending out review copies is an expensive business. When in doubt don't. Instead send a review copy request slip when you send out the press release.

It still astounds me that the review process can take as long as it does. It is not unusual for us to still be having books reviewed a year after the copies were sent out. Initially this may come as a bit of a disappointment but it has the very real benefit of keeping public attention alive over an extended time span.

the book launch

On the date of publication every "author" will expect there to be some sort of launch party to celebrate his or her new book. They will expect a goodly turnout from the Press – reviewers anxious to discover a new talent to laud through their columns – as well as local bookshop people and librarians. They will also expect to generate a large number of sales, willingly signing copies of the new book for all those guests who will naturally see this as an opportunity not to be missed. For the publisher to question the value of such an event will probably be seen as sheer heresy.

Launch parties can be fun. It is good to be able to celebrate the creation of a new book and to give the photographer the opportunity to have their moment of public glory. However, such launches rarely achieve what is expected by the "author" who will probably feel that the publisher has not really tried. It is very difficult to get significant attendance from the Press, even harder to get booksellers to come and so many of those special guests who had promised faithfully to attend never seem to materialise. And of course even the simplest event can turn out to be very expensive by the time that venue hire, cost of drinks, and invitation and mailing costs are taken into consideration. The budget that should be directed to a short run title can be totally consumed within a matter of hours and with very little lasting effect.

It is hardly surprising therefore that publishers may be resistant to the idea and try their utmost to dissuade you. If, however, you are able to persuade a publisher do not be put off if they are only willing to make a part contribution towards the costs. Do bear in mind that if the publisher pays then less money will be available for the future marketing of your book – if you pay then you will either be spending your advance or your future royalties.

The following should be borne in mind for all such launch parties:

- Be actively involved in all the arrangements.

- Try to tie in to another event. An exhibition opening would be ideal, or a talk that you are giving. Think of ways in which it could be of benefit to someone else who might be willing to pay or at least contribute towards costs.

- Choose the venue carefully. Always bear in mind location. If its difficult to get to people won't.

- Keep the mailing list small – sending to people who you could reasonably expect to attend.

- Don't be lavish with invitation cards unless you can persuade someone else to pay. Think about sending run-on jackets from the book and a simple personal letter as an alternative.

- Give people adequate notice. I would suggest that you send out the invitations about three weeks before the event and certainly no later than two weeks before. Don't leave things to chance. Do phone people up to remind them.

- Make sure that you have enough friends coming so that if no-one else arrives the event will not have been a total disaster.

- Be modest with the catering and if necessary do not be afraid of having a pay bar. You can always arrange to keep glasses topped up for your key guests. Try approaching a local wine merchant for sponsorship perhaps offering them the opportunity to run the event as a wine-tasting.

- Expect to sell no books. You may then be pleasantly surprised.

- Try to arrange for some photographs to be taken, particularly if you have any name guests. You may well be able to use the photographs later for press purposes.

- Do not be afraid to do it differently. There are no rules other than that you are trying to gain some press coverage and make the event enjoyable.

publication date

When the publication day comes first-time authors tend to believe that every bookshop will have their book in stock and on prominent display. There is one major problem with this. Bookshops must first buy stock and there is no way in which you can force them to do so. They have to be convinced that the book is going to sell and clearly unless considerable efforts have been made before publication date you are unlikely to find your title in many shops.

The publication date is not the date that you expect to receive finished copies of the book but is a notional date which you choose. Allow yourself plenty of leeway particularly if you plan a book launch. I can imagine nothing more embarrassing than holding a party to which the guest of honour, the new book, does not show up.

The larger publishers will always seek to have advance copies of a book well ahead of the publication date to enable pre-publication publicity to begin. They will want copies to send out to reviewers so that reviews can coincide with the publication date. They will also want their larger customers to see the title as early as possible.

Smaller publishers or self-publishers are rarely in such a good position.

catalogues and flyers

The self-publisher with just the single title is at a disadvantage in a number of ways not least in that they are not able to produce a catalogue which can be kept as reference by the booksellers. Most publishers will produce a catalogue at least once a year and ideally twice – one for the autumn selling period and one for the spring. They will aim for publication dates for these to be three months before the period. Prime space will be given to the new titles and these will usually be lavishly illustrated with extensive text. Older titles forming the backlist will often be presented as just the title plus a single short sentence. In preparing our own catalogue we take a slightly different approach. Whilst we provide a strong focus on the new titles we still see the backlist as important and we therefore try to include a cover photograph and a reasonable description for each book.

Flyers or leaflets are more appropriate for the one title publisher. However, before you decide to produce one think about what you want to use it for and determine the number that you are going to produce accordingly. If you are aiming to sell to both the book trade and to individuals then make sure that you produce two variants on the reverse of the flyer. The leaflet for individuals will need a simple order form whilst the one for the trade should indicate the discount structure that you are offering. Remember that the standard trade discount is 35% except for single copy orders which are usually supplied at 25% discount.

I take the view that if you are spending money on a flyer you should try to produce it to a quality that matches your book. Colour is obviously the most effective if you can afford it. If not try to get some dynamism into the design. Also always ensure that you include a picture of the book cover. Flyers can be very usefully deployed as inserts in magazines but if you are intending to do this calculate the costs first. On occasion you may find that it is cheaper to take advertising space than to produce however many thousand leaflets and pay for their insertion. As with all things related to advertising I try to analyse cost against realistic potential sales revenue.

paid advertising?

For the self-publisher with only a single title to sell paid advertising is rarely cost-effective. The same is true for small publishers. Space rates are relatively high even in the lower circulation magazines and are not always easy to justify simply in terms of the direct sales that you are likely to generate. There is only one way to really look at cost-effectiveness and that is on the basis of the following formula.

Advertisement Cost/Net Profit per copy = Units to be sold

The units to be sold should then be related back to the known circulation figures of the magazine. (Circulation figures themselves can sometimes be rather dubious. Always ask what the print run is or even better the sales per issue). If the units to be sold equates to 2% or less than the circulation then advertising should be cost effective. If, however, it is 10% or more you are simply going to lose money. The one possible exception to this rule is when a major part of the magazine is dedicated to a feature on your work, and even then I would be nervous if the "units to be sold" figure was much higher than 5% of circulation.

Assuming a net profit figure of £1.50 and a space rate of £150 the formula would work out as follows:-

£150 (Advertisement Cost)/£1.50 (Net Profit per copy) = 100 Units to be sold.

For the advert to be cost effective you would be looking for a circulation of 5,000.

There will always be occasions when you are tempted to ignore this formulaic approach. That is fine as long as you remain aware of it. If you want to advertise so that you reach a specific group (such as gallery curators) to try and increase your profile then there is no reason not to do so but do not confuse that with the task of trying to sell your book.

Always bear in mind the additional costs associated with placing an ad. These may include design costs, typesetting, special delivery etc and could well amount to a further 30% – 50% of the cost of the advertising space.

Given the above it is perhaps not surprising that many publishers are hesitant to place adverts for short-run photography books. This can be interpreted as a lack of commitment on the part of the publisher but is more likely to be a calculated assessment of the value of utilising limited resources in that particular direction.

what other media coverage can you aim for?

The press and the media will be able to consider a range of approaches.

- The local interest story

  Where were you born? Where did you go to school? Where do you work? Where do you live? If there are four different answers then you probably have at least four local papers which may be persuaded to do a story.

- The feature article

  Think about the hooks that might be sensible for a feature article. Anniversary dates; the publication of a government report on a given subject.

- A competition

  Competitions can be very effective across a range of media and at national and local levels. When making the arrangements check that the text to accompany the competition gives the information that you want to put across. Think about making the prize a bit more special. Signed copies of your book is a standard way.

- Readers offers

  Special offers to readers of appropriate magazines can be an effective way both of getting coverage for the book and also selling direct copies where you will lose less discount. Remember to be careful about any breach of the Net Book Agreement.

- A photo opportunity

  Always think in terms of what might make a photo opportunity and don't be depressed that you can't get a press photographer there. Take your own photographs or get someone else to. Laying out and editing 150 photographs in a hired church hall, the first printed sheets coming off the presses, receiving the first bound copies, the book launch, the book signing are all opportunities for coverage in a local or regional paper.

- The news story

  It is news if you receive an Arts Council grant or some other form of sponsorship. Use it as an opportunity to get coverage and ensure that you include information about the book.

- The diary comment

  If you don't get the grant but still intend to proceed then turn it into a diary story.

Many of these suggestions are geared towards local and regional press. Don't ignore these as they can be highly effective. At worst they can give a warm feeling of celebrity – at best they can achieve some real sales. We all want reviews in the national press but be realistic – there are literally hundreds of books challenging for this limited space every week of the year.

mailing lists

Building mailing lists takes time. We work on the basis that there are a number of different key categories and that even these can be split down further into sub categories such as Local, Regional, National, International, Specialist, Non-Specialist.

- Press and Media
- Bookshops
- Galleries
- Libraries
- Individuals

The best lists are of those who have bought books from you previously. Unfortunately this is not a lot of help for the first time publisher.

List rental is frequently used. This is the purchase of addressed labels for a one-off use only. There are a massive range of lists available for rental but until you use one you have no way of really judging its effectiveness. You should also be aware that there may well be duplication across lists.

It always makes sense to try to test a list. Our approach when we are using new lists is to select a starter number – perhaps as few as fifty or a hundred names if the list is specialist – mail to these and wait for the results before mailing the full list. On such a list we would be looking for a response of perhaps even as high as 5%. On a less defined, yet still specialist list the response could be expected to be 2% or lower. At this rate of response postage costs may outweigh the return but this may still make sense for the publisher if they are trying to build a list of future potential purchasers. For the self-publisher with the single title the important point is the immediate financial result. You should never forget that you must analyse the response in terms of the financial return.

When you are developing your lists for the press and the media it is essential that you try to find out names as well as organisations. This is particularly valuable when dealing with the larger organisations. It is for example next to worthless to send a review copy or a press release to the Literary Editor of a national newspaper if you are trying to get them to cover the book as a feature or hoping that they might just use a single image from the book. Don't expect your book to be passed across internally to the right person. You will almost certainly be waiting a very long time.

direct sales

Direct sales are particularly attractive to any publisher. It is easy to understand why. Opposite is a comparison between the return to a publisher from sales to a bookshop at standard discounts and the return through direct sales.

discounts lost and costs incurred – single copy

	Standard	Direct Mail
Retailer's Discount	25.00%	0.00%
Sales Rep Commission	9.37%	0.00%
Distribution	5.25%	7.00%
Postage & Packing	10.00%	10.00%
Total	49.62%	17.00%
Return to Publisher	50.38%	83.00%

Assuming that the book in question retails at £10.00 then you will see that in this example we would be £3.26 better off selling through direct mail than through single orders to the trade.

The commission for sales reps and the distribution costs are both charged as a percentage of the invoice value after trade discount has been given. In this instance the bookshop is being invoiced at £7.50 for the book.

discounts lost and costs incurred – general sales

If the order for this copy of the book is part of a larger order then the scenario changes again as follows.

	Standard	Direct Mail
Retailer's Discount	35.00%	0.00%
Sales Rep Commission	8.12%	0.00%
Distribution	4.55%	7.00%
Postage & Packing	7.00%	10.00%
Total	54.67%	17.00%
Return to Publisher	45.33%	83.00%

Again assuming that the book in question retails at £10.00 then you will see that in this example we would be £3.77 better off selling through direct mail than through the trade.

Notice that in this example the commission for sales reps and the distribution costs are both charged at a lower percentage. This is because the charge is based on the invoice value after trade discount has been given, which in this instance means an invoice value for the book of £6.50. Also notice that there is a reduced postage and packing cost simply because unit costs reduce if you are able to consolidate a number of books together in one package.

It is clear from both these examples just how attractive direct sale can be to a publisher. Obviously if you wish to make a special offer to the direct mail purchaser this will reduce the return you generate but by looking at these figures you can see that if an offer of a 30% discount were made you would still be seeing a better return than could be generated through the trade sale. There are other advantages to direct mail.

- You can set up a pre-publication offer. This will help to raise some of the cash necessary to pay the printing bill. If you make your offer say two months before publication date then you may have three or even four months of active income generation before your bills are due for payment. Selling through the trade you would expect to receive no income back until at least a month after the publication date.

- Payment is received before the book is dispatched. This provides not only a great boost to your cash flow but also avoids any possibility of non-payment which is an increasing risk with regard to sales made on credit through the trade.

- Generally there will be less administration. You probably won't need to provide an invoice and you certainly won't need to prepare monthly statements or any follow-up correspondence for chasing money etc.

- You will be establishing a list of known buyers of books which may prove to be a solid customer base for any future projects in which you are engaged.

contracts

For many photographers, and indeed authors generally, the offer to have a book published is a bit like winning the pools – something to be celebrated not questioned. It is very easy to be swept along by the excitement. Having got this far few people want to jeopardise things in any way. Asking for a contract is for many people a bit like talking about money – rather embarrassing and something that they feel distinctly uncomfortable about.

Any agreement to publish your work should be confirmed with a written contract that details all the terms and conditions that will apply. It doesn't matter that you trust every word that your publisher says or even that they are your closest friend, your brother or your sister, a contract is still vital.

It is important to realise that by entering into such an agreement you will be relinguishing considerable rights over your work for a very long time. Copyright will remain yours but the right to publish the work in book form will probably, with some exclusions, have been handed over for the period of that copyright. You should also realise that things change. The individual that you have dealt with may move on to another job or be run over by a bus or, equally traumatic, the publishing house may be taken over by another company with little affinity to your work.

It is also important that the contract is entered into at an early stage to allow plenty of time to consider and negotiate the terms on offer. As a general rule we try to issue a draft contract as soon as we have agreed that we are going to publish the work. Whilst each contract follows a standard format we recognise that no situation is identical and we therefore try to accommodate the concerns of each photographer as far as possible.

Few people find contracts easy to follow. If you receive a contract and don't fully understand the terms and the implications then you should ask the publisher for further clarification, or seek professional legal advice. Don't sign if you don't understand.

The following is a copy of the sort of contract that we would normally issue. In italics, under each of the numbered clauses, I have tried to offer further explanation.

CORNERHOUSE PUBLICATIONS   70 Oxford Street, Manchester M1 5NH
Contract Number_____

MEMORANDUM OF AGREEMENT made this   day of   19   between

(The "Photographer") of the one part

and

CORNERHOUSE PUBLICATIONS of 70 Oxford Street, Manchester M1 5NH

(The "Publishers") of the other part.

(The expressions "Photographer" and "Publishers" shall, where the context admits, include the executors, administrators and assigns or successors in business as the case may be).

In the event of the death of the photographer the contract continues to remain in force and becomes the property of their estate for the period of copyright. For the publisher the contract is an asset of the company which may be transferred or sold to another company.

WHEREBY it is mutually agreed as follows concerning a work original to the Photographer and provisionally entitled

(hereinafter called the "Work").

1. In consideration of the payments hereinafter mentioned, the Photographer hereby grants to the Publishers the sole and exclusive right and licence to produce and publish and themselves further to license the Work or any abridgement of the Work or any substantial part of the Work in volume form in all languages for the legal term of copyright throughout the World, subject to the conditions following.

Whilst the photographer retains copyright they have agreed to pass over (to assign) all the publishing rights detailed in the contract to the publisher.

The Photographer undertakes that he/she will not during the continuance of this Agreement without the consent of the Publishers prepare otherwise than for the Publishers any work of a nature which may reasonably be considered to affect prejudicially the sales of the Work.

An example of this could be a retrospective book which included all or the majority of the images in this book.

2. The Publishers shall publish the Work at their own expense and unless prevented by circumstances outside their control within a reasonable time of signature of this Agreement.

It is useful to include a fixed time period, perhaps eighteen months. It can be argued that lack of money is a reason outside the control of the publisher.

While proper care will be taken of the Work, the Publishers shall not be responsible for any loss or damage to it while it is in the Publishers' possession or in the course of production or in transit.

Always ensure that you get proper insurance cover. Never send original material that you do not have in duplicate form.

3. Written permission to use any copyright material not original to the Photographer for which permission is required shall be obtained for all languages and editions which are the subject of this Agreement by the Photographer who agrees to bear all fees for the use of such material or promptly reimburse the Publishers for any fees paid by them in respect of such copyright material.

The photographer is expected to pay any charges for the use of material which is not their own and to make contact with the copyright holder to get their written agreement that the material can be used. This may apply to any introductory text, any quotations and any illustrations. Often however the publisher will agree to take on these responsibilities.

The Photographer undertakes to read, check and correct the proofs and to return them to the Publishers within fourteen days of their receipt, failing which the Publishers may consider them passed for press. The cost of all alterations made by the Photographer in the finished artwork and in the proofs (other than the correction of printers' errors) above ten per cent of the original cost of composition shall be borne by the Photographer. Should any charge arise under this clause the amount may be deducted from any sum which may become due to the Photographer under this Agreement.

This puts the onus on the photographer to check everything. It ensures that in the event of mistakes the photographer can have no come back against the publisher. By making the photographer financially responsible for changes it helps to ensure that last minute rewrites or other changes are kept to an absolute minimum.

5. The Photographer hereby warrants to the Publishers that he/she has full power to make this Agreement, that he/she is the sole Photographer of the Work and is the owner of the rights herein granted, that the Work is original to him/her, and has not previously been published in volume form in the territories covered by this Agreement, that the Work is in no way whatever an infringement of any existing copyright or licence, that it contains nothing obscene, libellous or defamatory, and that all statements contained therein purporting to be facts are to the best of the Photographer's knowledge and belief true. The Photographer will indemnify and keep the Publishers indemnified against all actions, suits, proceedings, claims, demands, damages and costs (including any legal costs or expenses properly incurred and any compensation costs or disbursements paid by the Publishers on the advice of their legal advisers to compromise or settle any claim) occasioned to the Publishers in consequence of any breach of this warranty or arising out of any claim alleging that the Work constitutes an infringement of copyright or contains libellous or defamatory matter, and the Photographer furthermore undertakes that he/she and his/her legal representatives will pay to the Publishers the cost of all copies withdrawn or destroyed and for any revisions to existing copies. The Publishers reserve the right to insist that the Photographer alter the text of the Work in such a way as may appear to them appropriate for the purpose of removing any passage which on the advice of the Publishers' legal advisers may be considered objectionable or likely to be actionable by law, but any such alteration or removal shall be without prejudice to and shall not affect the Photographer's liability under his/her warranty and indemnity herein contained.

This is a very important clause for the photographer to consider. You are confirming that the work is your own and that you have full power to enter into this contract. You are also confirming that there is nothing in the content of the book that could lead to legal action against the publishers and that in the case of such legal action you are accepting the financial responsibility. In addition you are agreeing to cover the publisher's costs in the event of copies of the book having to be destroyed or amended.

The Publisher is also asserting the right to make changes to the book which they deem necessary to avoid legal action being taken.

This is always a very worrying clause for photographers. It suggests some terrifying scenarios. If you have any reason whatsoever to believe that your work may have the sort of consequences outlined then it is essential to get good legal advice at an early stage.

6. The published price of the first United Kingdom edition of the Work shall be approximately

£   per paperback edition £   per hardback edition

This is a preliminary indication to give you an idea of the likely income that will be generated through royalties.

The Publishers shall have the power in their discretion to alter the published price of the first or any subsequent edition as they may think fit and, in not less than three years after the first publication, to sell part or the whole of the residue at a reduced price, or as a remainder at the best prices that such remainder stock will fetch. The Publishers shall give the Photographer first refusal of purchasing the remainder stock. Such option shall be sufficiently complied with on the Publishers' part by posting to the Photographer at his/her last known address an offer of such remainder stock, and this offer shall be deemed to be refused if no reply is received by the Publishers within four weeks after posting such offer.

Another important clause. It allows the publisher to control pricing. It also clarifies the company's policy with regard to remaindering their books. In this instance no books will be remaindered in the three years following publication.

Equally important, the photographer has the first option to buy stock prior to it being offered to a remainder merchant.

Photographers should always ensure that a clause covering these points is included.

7. Subject to the terms and conditions set out in this Agreement, the Publishers shall make to the Photographer the following payments in

respect of all copies of the Work sold:

a) HOME HARDBOUND SALES

On the British published price of all copies sold, excluding such copies as may be subject to subsequent provisions of this Agreement, or as otherwise mutually agreed, be sold subject to a different royalty:
    10%
On reprints of 1000 copies or less:
    7.5%

b) PUBLISHERS' OWN PAPERBACKS
On all copies sold from the first print run a royalty on the British published price of:
    7.5% on all copies sold in the home market
    7.5% on all copies sold in the export market.

c) BOOK CLUBS AND SPECIAL DISCOUNT SALES
On all copies sold as Bulk Sales of 100 copies or more at a discount of 60% or more, whether at home or for overseas, a royalty on the British published price of:
    5%

d) OTHER EDITIONS
On all copies sold under licence by the publishers:
    50% of the net amounts received by the Publishers

e) ROYALTY-INCLUSIVE SALES
On all copies sold bound or in sheets for the purpose of publication in the USA or elsewhere:
    50% of the net amounts received by the Publishers

f) MECHANICAL REPRODUCTION
In the event of the Publishers reproducing the Work in complete or substantially complete form by film micrography, reprographic reproduction, videotapes, film strips, or by means of any other contrivance whether by sight or sound or a combination of both, whether now in existence or hereinafter invented. Reproduction for use as part of or in conjunction with a cinematograph film or television broadcast is excluded:
    7.5% on the British published price

This clause specifies the royalties that you will be paid. The royalties clause is essentially about the sale of products by the publisher. The following clause relates to the sale of rights ie. the ability of others to produce. The level of royalty will depend on the form in which the book is sold. Further detail on this is provided later in this chapter.

A higher % can usually be agreed for a reprint as long as the edition size is adequate.

GENERAL PROVISO
Provided that no royalties shall be paid on copies of the Work sold at cost or less, presented to the Photographer, to the Press or to others, lost through theft or damaged or destroyed by fire, water, natural disasters, enemy action, acts of civil war, acts of terrorism/freedom-fighting, in transit or otherwise.

Put simply this means that you will only receive a royalty on copies sold at a profit. There is potential for confusion and evasion in this clause particularly around what is the cost price of the book.

8. The sale of the following rights shall be negotiated on behalf of the Photographer by the Publishers and the Photographer hereby grants the said rights to the Publishers during the term of this Agreement. The Publishers shall pay to the Photographer the following percentages of the gross amounts received in payment for such rights:

a) Mechanical reproduction rights (ie the right to produce or reproduce the Work in complete or substantially complete form or to license its reproduction of the Work by film micrography, reprographic reproduction, videotapes, film strips, or by means of any other contrivance whether by sight or sound or a combination of both, whether now in existence or hereinafter invented, EXCEPT in so far as reproduction is for use as part of or in conjunction with a cinematograph film or television broadcast)
50%

b) Reprint rights
50%

c) The right of publication in the USA
50%

d) Translation rights
        50%

The rights mentioned in this clause will not be disposed of by the Publishers except with the consent of the Photographer which shall not be unreasonably withheld. All rights not hereby granted to the Publisher are reserved by the Photographer, including the Public Lending Right.

This clause specifies the payments that you will receive from the sale of particular rights. Further detail on rights is provided later in this chapter

9. The paper, printing, binding, jackets or covers and embellishments, the promotion, the manner and extent of the advertisement, the number and distribution of free copies for the Press or otherwise, the reprinting, pricing and terms of sale of the first and any subsequent edition of the Work issued by the Publishers, and the negotiation of subsidiary rights under this Agreement, shall be in the sole discretion of the Publishers, who shall in other respects (except only as herein provided) have the entire control of the publication. Any specific agreements with regard to the specification for design and production will be provided in a rider to this memorandum.

This is confirming who is in charge. The last sentence is our own addition and allows for clarification of the level of involvement that we expect from the photographer in a separate rider to the contract.

10. The Publishers shall render the first account of the Work as at 31 March next following the date of first publication and subsequently at 31 March annually, and all monies due to the Photographer shall be paid to him/her within two months of the said accountancy dates provided, however, that no account need be submitted unless specifically demanded nor payment made in respect of any year in which the sum due is less than £10, in which case the amount will be carried forward to the next accountancy date.

This clarifies the process of royalty payment. For reasons of administrative simplicity we currently pay royalties on an annual basis. Some publishers pay six-monthly or even quarterly.

The Publishers agree to pay the Photographer in advance and on account of sums that may become due to the Photographer under this Agreement the sum of £XXX of which £XXX is payable on signature of this Agreement by both the Publishers and the Photographer and the balance of £XXX on date of publication. In the event of the Publishers not proceeding to publication for whatever reason any amounts paid as an advance to the Photographer will not be returnable.

Our advance payments are generally very small simply because we can not afford to front load the costs of producing a book. Larger publishers should be expected to make significant advance payments. It is not unusual to receive between 50% and 100% of all the royalties that would be due from the full print run of the first edition.

11. The Photographer shall not during the continuance of this Agreement, without the consent of the Publishers, publish any abridgement or part of the Work in volume form, nor shall the Photographer prepare otherwise than for the Publishers any work which reproduces in identical or similar form any considerable part of the Work.

This to a large extent repeats the commitment made in clause 1.

12. The Photographer shall be entitled to receive on publication ten complimentary copies of the paperback edition of the Work; and shall have the right to purchase for personal use copies of the Work on trade terms. The Photographer shall be entitled to receive three copies of any hardcover edition issued under licence from the Publishers and of any subsequent edition produced by the Publishers. The Photographer shall be given the option for four weeks of purchasing remaindered copies at the remainder price, such option to be made under the terms of Clause 6 above.

This specifies the number of free copies that you will receive. You should receive complimentary copies of every edition published. We also allow photographers to purchase books for themselves. We generally allow these to be sold in controlled situations such as workshops or other personal appearance situations. The sale of books to any trade outlet is unacceptable as it would be in direct competition with the publisher.

The photographer's option to purchase remaindered copies is also restated.

13. The copyright in the Work rests in the Photographer, and the Publishers

shall as and where appropriate take all available steps to protect the same in the name of the Photographer in accordance with the provisions of the Universal Copyright Convention.

This confirms the copyright position. You must always ensure that this is absolutely clearly stated in the contract.

14. If at any time the Publishers allow the Work to go out of print or off the market in all editions issued by the Publishers or authorised by them and if within twelve months of having received a written request from the Photographer to do so they have not reprinted and placed on the market a new edition or authorised the same then all rights granted under this Agreement shall forthwith and without further notice revert to the Photographer (but not those deriving from the option of Clause 18 hereof) without prejudice to all rights of the Publishers in respect of any contracts or negotiations properly entered into by them with any third party prior to the date of such reversion and without prejudice to any monies already paid or then due to the Photographer from the Publishers. The Photographer's requirements that the Work be reprinted shall be regarded as satisfied if at the time of the Photographer's giving notice the Publishers have subleased rights for an edition scheduled for publication within twelve months of such notice being given.

The publisher has the right to allow the book to go out of print. There is no requirement for them to produce a second edition if they do not wish to. Once they are out of stock of the book then the photographer can make a written request for a reprint. If, at the end of twelve months, a new edition has not been printed then the rights for the book revert back to the photographer. This means that they can approach another publisher or publish the book themselves if they so wish.

16. If the Publishers at any time by themselves or anyone acting on their behalf wilfully fail to comply with any of the conditions accepted by them in this Agreement within one month after written notification from the Photographer of such failure, or should the Publishers be bankrupt, this Agreement shall thereupon determine and the Photographer shall be free to license any other person, firm or company to print and publish the Work or otherwise deal in or dispose of any or all rights in the copyright therein, notwithstanding anything to the contrary contained or implied in any part of this Agreement.

You have the right to hold the publishers to their contractual obligations. If they fail to comply you have the right to give a month's written notice of the problem and withdraw from the contract if there is no change in their approach. You can do this on any points which are covered in the contract.

17. The Publishers shall have the first refusal of the Photographer's next work suitable for publication in volume form, and the Photographer shall offer the Publishers for this purpose the same rights and territories as those covered by this Agreement. Such work shall be the subject of a fresh agreement between the Photographer and the Publishers on terms that shall be fair and reasonable. If no terms have been agreed for the publication of the work within eight weeks of its submission to the Publisher the Photographer shall be at liberty to enter into an agreement with any other publisher for its publication provided that the Photographer shall not subsequently accept from anyone else for that work less favourable terms than are offered by the Publishers.

The publisher will have invested a considerable amount of money in your book. If it or you becomes a success they will wish, not unreasonably, to benefit from that success. Consequently they will expect to have first option on your next book. For photography books this is rarely a significant clause though we generally retain it. I tend to take a rather pragmatic view, however. If the relationship has been good for the photographer they will wish to remain with the same publisher. If it has been a difficult one then holding them to a contractual clause is not likely to augur well for the next project.

18. The Author hereby asserts his moral right to be identified as the author of the Work, and the Publishers undertake

a) to print with due prominence on every edition of the Work published by themselves the words "The right of "Photographer X" to be identified as author of this work has been asserted by him in accordance with the Copyright, Designs and Patents Act 1988".

b) to make it a condition of contract with any licensee concerning any edition of the Work to be published in the United Kingdom that a notice of assertion in the same terms as the above shall be printed with due prominence in every edition published by or further licensed by such Licensee.

This clause is essentially to protect your right to be identified and credited as the originator of the work.

19. If any difference shall arise between the Photographer and the Publishers touching the meaning of this Agreement or the rights and liabilities of the parties thereto, it shall be referred to the arbitration of two persons (one to be named by each party) or their mutually agreed umpire, in accordance with the provision of the Arbitration Act 1950 or any amending or substituted statute for the time being in force.

It makes sense to try to resolve disagreement through arbitration in preference to going through the courts.

20. This Agreement shall be governed by and interpreted in all respects in accordance with the Laws of England.

SIGNED .... Photographer/Author

SIGNED .... for the Publishers

I would not offer this contract as any particular model of good practice but rather as an example of the type of concerns that you should expect to find covered in a publisher's contract. Contracts inevitably vary from publisher to publisher. You should also realise that most contracts are designed for literary rather than visual works and therefore you may come across some rather odd clauses. As I have said, when in doubt question and never sign until you are absolutely certain that you understand what is being asked of you.

There are other things on which you should seek clarification. We tend to include them in a rider to a contract.

standards of production

You will be concerned to ensure that if a publisher has promised duotone reproduction that is what you will get. What recourse will there be if they inform you at a late stage that the work will be in single black only? Every aspect of production that you agree should be detailed and you should expect it to form part of the contract.

sponsorship

Who is empowered to seek sponsorship and who receives the benefit? Are you able to veto sponsorship from a company that you feel to be inappropriate?

expenses

Will any contribution be made to your out-of-pocket expenses in working with the publisher? These will involve everything from postage, faxes, telephone calls through to travel or hotel costs if you are to attend the printing. We would normally agree a fixed sum which we would expect to cover only part of the costs involved.

design

What control, if any, will you have of the design process? It is unlikely that a publisher would give you more than a consultative role but check to what extent this will operate.

cost of prints

Who will pay for the cost of making the prints for the book? This is always a difficult one. Whilst making prints will cost money the prints will be returned to you after the printing process. There will usually be some very minor damage to at least a few of the prints though this will often be no more than slightly worn edges or corners. They may not be resaleable but they will generally be in good enough condition for reuse as exhibition prints. Given this, I take the view that it is unreasonable to expect the publisher to cover the full cost of prints.

Ultimately this will become an area for negotiation but that negotiation should take place at the same time as the contract is signed. We will normally seek to pay part of any agreed cost for this through the provision of additional complimentary copies of the book for the photographer.

purchase of copies

If you are being offered the right to purchase books for personal use you need to know the terms under which you can buy them.

rights

Rights are a complicated issue that should not be ignored. Faced with a contract you will be presented with a list of rights which are either being assigned to the publisher or which they wish to handle on your behalf. Even if you have heard the terminology before their implications may not be clear.

Essentially rights fall into in two categories – volume rights and subsidiary rights.

volume rights

Volume rights are all the rights that the publisher might reasonably and realistically expect to control and utilise as part of the agreement to publish. They are usually subject to royalty payment rather than lump sum payment. In the contract shown they are the rights referred to in Clause 7. They are seen as those rights which most directly relate to the publication which is envisaged. They allow the publisher to produce the work as a printed book but they may also make allowance for developing technology such as the production of the book in a video format or as an electronic book. Essentially volume rights are those in which either the publisher is involved directly in the production of the end product or has licensed that production process to another publisher.

Volume rights are seen as being central to the publishing contract and under the control of the publisher without the need for reference to the author for permission to assign them. There are other rights which may or may not be granted to the publisher. These are called subsidiary rights.

subsidiary rights

- Mechanical reproduction

  These are increasingly seen as part of the volume rights. It is the right to produce or licence the production of the work by film micrography, reprographic reproduction, videotape, film strip or similar means. Generally there is a statement which seeks to cover any future technological development which might form the basis for presenting the work in an alternative form to the book. These rights are not intended to cover television or film and these should be considered separately if there is a potential for exploitation.

- Electronic publication

  With developments in technology this is an increasingly justifiable exertion of volume rights. Previously it has tended to refer to database usage and incorporation in software.

- First serial rights

  The right to publish extracts of the book usually in a magazine before the book is published.

- Second serial rights

  The right to publish extracts of the book usually in a magazine after the book has been published.
- One-shot periodical rights

  The right to publish the whole work in a magazine or book in one issue. This more usually applies to fiction.

- Digest and condensation rights

  The right to publish the whole work in an abridged form.

- Paperback rights

  Some publishers publish primarily in hardback. This right allows them to license others to produce a paperback of the work.

- Book Club rights

  Apart from selling copies of a book to a book club a publisher may wish to license a book club to produce its own club edition of the book.

- Same language territorial rights

  Co-editions can be very important for the viability of books and particularly for illustrated books with high production costs. Even though the USA and the UK share a common language it is often best for a US edition to be produced. This is most usually done through a US publisher who joins with the lead publisher at the initial production stage. This results in larger print runs being possible and consequently a lower unit price being achieved. Both editions are almost identical with changes generally being limited to imprint details. This also covers the right to reprint an existing book.

- Translation rights

  This is very much the same as the previous rights. It allows co-editions to be entered into and reprints to be undertaken in a different language.

- Merchandising rights

  Rarely thought of as likely to have any value in connection with a photography book but think of postcards, greetings cards, posters.

  If the publisher is willing to search out these markets for you it may be worth considering.

With subsidiary rights the publishers generally require the consent of the photographer though this should not be unreasonably withheld. All rights not granted to the publisher are reserved by the photographer. The Public Lending Right is one of these.

For all these rights the photographer will receive payment only when the rights are called upon, ie when they are sold to a third party. They will all be subject to a percentage return to the photographer and you should think carefully about the percentage that you agree. You should however recognise that it will be the publisher who is doing the work in selling the rights and that this may involve a high level of expenditure. There is no point in achieving a 95% share of income if the end result is that the publisher doesn't feel it worthwhile to try to sell the rights concerned.

The publisher also has rights. The design, layout and the typography are all elements which the publisher has undertaken and financed and which have no connection to the copyright material. It is therefore legitimate for the publisher to make a charge for the reproduction of this as separate to the content. Any income from this is not shared with the photographer.

distribution contracts

If you decide to use a trade distributor always ensure that you either have a distribution contract or a letter confirming in detail the terms of your agreement.

The following points are those that you should ensure are properly covered

- Ownership

  It must be clearly stated that all books remain the property of the publisher.

- The charge

  Normally this will be a percentage of the invoice value. You could expect to pay anything between 6% and 8% for a service which would simply covering storage and the physical packing and distribution. As well as this percentage you would also pay all the postage costs incurred. Additional services such as sales representation, marketing, invoicing and cash collection would add considerably to this cost. As a general rule of thumb you should expect a full distribution service to give you a return of between 40% and 45% of the retail price of a book.

- Payment terms

  Accounts will be made up monthly and you will be required to pay the distributor within 30 days if they are not collecting payments for you. This will mean that you are invariably paying the distributor before you are receiving the income from the sales of the books.

  If the distributor is collecting cash on your behalf then expect the terms to be that you will be paid 90 days after the month of the invoice.

- Territory

  What countries will your distributor be handling? If the distributor is simply handling physical distribution on your behalf then there is no reason for concern. If, however, they are offering a sales service across a broad geographical region then you must be very careful to research what is on offer. Do they have sufficient reps in the field to offer the service that they are suggesting ? If in doubt always ask for references from other publishers working with that distributor.

- Exclusive or non-exclusive

  Will they be the sole distributors in those countries? This really only applies if they are undertaking sales on your behalf. Only agree exclusive terms if you are absolutely certain that they are the right distributor for you. If you can, keep your options open by agreeing non-exclusive terms.

- Discounts to be offered

If your distributor is undertaking the selling then you should agree what discount structure you are willing to offer to the bookshops.

- Period of notice

I would suggest that you should never agree to a contract which requires more than six months notice to terminate unless as part of that contract the distributor is making a significant marketing commitment. In such an instance it would be reasonable to agree a twelve month notice period.

- Method of delivery

It makes sense to find out the method of delivery used and the standard charge. Most distributors will use a contract delivery service for which there will be a fixed charge for UK deliveries.

It also makes sense to get some clarification of delivery schedules. It will not do you a lot of good with the bookshops if your distributor is taking three weeks to get around to despatch. You should expect the turnaround period to be no more than three or four working days from receipt of the invoice at the warehouse.

- Insurance

Who is responsible for providing insurance cover for the stock whilst it is with the distributor? It is normal for the publisher to be responsible for this.

- Free copies

Normally a distributor will take a percentage of the invoice value. What happens when you want them to send out press copies or other complimentary copies? Always ensure that you agree a fixed price for this. You should expect it to be about 25p plus postage.

- Special deliveries

This is rather like free copies. What will happen if you want to arrange a delivery of a large number of copies – perhaps for an exhibition opening? Will they charge the fixed percentage? This would work out at a very high charge if you were sending 200 copies of a book to a gallery. If for example it was at an invoice value of £10 per book you could end up paying perhaps £140 for the privilege of your distributor putting together one large package. Clearly this would be an unreasonable charge, particularly as you would still have to pay all the postage costs involved.

- Bad debt

Normally you would expect to be responsible for any bad debt no matter who is undertaking the invoicing. Whilst it is not unreasonable for you to require all new accounts to pay for their first order through a pro-forma invoice there are many outlets that would be unwilling to take stock except on standard credit terms.

If you are in direct control of the sales reps then you can determine whether or not to agree credit. If, however, the distributor is responsible for this, then remember that it is in their own interests to ensure that bad debt is minimised. You may not get paid but neither will they.

- Stock variation

The distributor may wish to include a clause that allows for some stock shrinkage. This should be kept to an absolute minimum. They should be required to check stock deliveries on arrival at their warehouse and notify you of quantities. If there is any variation from the delivery note given by the printer this should be reported immediately so that you can make a claim against the printer.

We all know that shrinkage, as it is politely termed, does happen, but if the initial delivery is correct then any shrinkage is almost certainly the result of theft or of despatch errors and is then surely the responsibility of the warehouse. I would certainly never agree to shrinkage levels of more than 0.5%.

- Stock checks

  You should ensure that the agreement allows for adequate stock checks. I would suggest these be undertaken on a quarterly basis.

- Extra charges

  It is always useful to agree the basis on which any additional charges will be levied. For example, if you want leaflets to be inserted or stickers to be added, how will they fix their charges? Remember that once the stock is with them you may have to agree almost anything they say so try to sort it out beforehand.

- Legal liability

  Expect your distributor to seek indemnity from you to cover any legal action. For example libellous or obscene material. They will quite reasonably expect you to take on board all the costs that might result from such an action.

money matters

If you finally decide to become a self-publisher rather than publishing through an existing house then your most difficult barrier is likely to be money. You are not alone. This is also the problem for the publisher – how to finance all the development and production costs on a project that, at best, can not be expected to return a profit for at least a year.

We looked earlier at the process of building up the estimate request for the printer and looked at the form of quotation that we might receive. This is one element in the task of building up a realistic budget.

The importance of sensible and realistic budgeting can not be underestimated. The following are the key budget heads that you should be looking at.

- Design fees

    Always get a firm price agreed with a designer. Confirm what additional costs you may be liable for. These may include materials, couriers, faxes etc. Confirm what documentation will be provided to you to justify these additional costs and agree a process of notification. I would suggest that extras should always be invoiced on a monthly basis so that you can keep a very close eye on how expenditure is going.

    Agree also on the timing of payments and any credit terms.

- Artwork production

    If typesetting or finished artwork production are not covered within the design fees then ensure that you get realistic estimates for these costs. Whilst they can be hard to quantify you will usually find that you can get a quote based on a per page rate.

- Reproduction fees and permissions

  If you are using work from anyone else that might need copyright clearance – quotes, images etc – try to get it early and get a price for it.

- Writer's fee

  Again agree this early. Work to a fixed fee and agree payment terms.

- Production costs

  These are all the costs associated with repro, printing, and binding. Agree any changes to your specification in writing along with any changes in cost that will result. Ensure that everything is covered within the quote. For example, is delivery included?

- Expenses

  Make a sensible allocation for all the expenses that you are likely to incur. List everything you can think of from phone calls and faxes through to delivery costs for the artwork. Don't forget to provide for overseeing the printing and allow for travel and accommodation costs.

- Finance costs

  If you are borrowing any money at all then make sure that you include proper allowance for the cost of that borrowing. Even if you are getting an interest-free loan or putting in your own cash it is sensible to include a calculation of the true cost of that finance. If you use £3000 of your own money over a one year period you will be losing perhaps £250 in interest.

- Marketing and publicity

  Allocate a budget that you believe works for the project and stick to it. Don't forget that even free publicity costs money in terms of the photocopying of press releases and AI sheets and don't forget about postage costs.

- Contingency

  Always include a contingency sum. I would suggest a minimum of 5% of the total budget. Don't treat it as a budget heading for non-essential expenditure and only use it when it is absolutely necessary.

the cost of selling

It is very easy to make wrong and potentially disastrous assumptions about book pricing. 2000 copies at a retail price of £10.00 may seem to give a retail value of £20,000 but there are a myriad of costs, commissions and discounts to be set against this.

The actual return from your 2000 copies is nowhere near this magic figure of £20,000.

Here is a breakdown of what you might realistically expect

Print run 2000 copies

Allowance for press copies, samples to sales reps and distributors, copyright deposit and other complimentary copies 150 copies
Balance of copies for sale 1850 copies
Maximum retail value 1850 books @ £10.00 = £18,500

	% of retail price
Standard bookshop discount (35%)	35.00%
Sales reps commission (12.5% of invoice value)	8.12%
Warehousing & distribution (7% of invoice value)	4.55%
Postage and packing (8.5% of retail value)	8.50%
% lost in direct sales costs	56.17%
Cash return after direct sales costs	£8,108.55

For the publisher who is paying a royalty (say of 7.5% of retail value) there is a further cost on every sale of 75p bringing the cash return down to £6,721.05.

If we compare this back to the original figure of £20,000 we will see that we have achieved a return of 33.6% (40.5% if there is no royalty). All of this assumes that you will sell every copy of the book and that is rarely as easy as it might seem. And, of course, it is before we have covered any of the production and development costs or any of the overheads involved.

There are a number of further factors that can reduce this return even further.

- If your book is being bought by a wholesaler they will be looking for a discount of around 50% rather than the booksellers' standard 35%.

- Many of the larger bookshop chains are now asking for higher discount. Some may ask for as much as 40% – 45%.

- Increasingly books are being bought on a returns basis, ie if the bookshop can not sell the book within a reasonable period (often less than six months) they will return it and expect to be either credited or reimbursed. Returned stock should never be accepted unless it is in fully resaleable condition with no visible signs of damage or handling whatsoever. The problem about this is that whilst you may be able to resell the book you will already have paid the distribution and postage and packing costs when you sent it out the first time around.

  If you have a good relationship with your reps they will probably allow you credit on their commission.

- Bad Debt

  However careful you are there will be occasions when you simply do not get paid. Again you will have already paid out for all the distribution costs. In the example above if you are not paid for 50 copies then you will lose £325. This will come straight off the bottom line and will reduce your percentage return.

  It is not, however, all gloom and doom. There are other ways in which you will be able to generate a better return.

- Single copy orders will usually attract a lower discount (25%)

though the postage cost will work out as a higher percentage cost.

- Direct sales to individuals won't incur any discount unless you decide to offer one.

- Direct sales to libraries will only require a discount of between 10% and 20%.

- Quantity sales may lose you more discount but you will save on postage.

  Given the high costs involved in selling a book it is hardly surprising that many self-publishers go it alone and handle everything. To do so requires not just time and energy but considerable amounts of bubble-wrap, jiffy bags, brown paper and tape, as well a good, dry storage area. You also need to have a particular temperament with good selling skills and the ability to cope with frequent rejection.

and so how do you price your book?

As a standard rule, commercial publishers will always be looking to mark up the retail price of a book at anything from four to eight times the production cost. It is easy to understand why from the figures that I have indicated. For most photography books, however, there is no way that these sort of mark ups can be achieved on a short print run of 2000 or so. Increasing the print run to reduce the unit price is also rarely a sensible option unless you have solid market research to indicate higher sales or, preferably, you have a financial backer.

Ultimately you must price the book at a level that people will pay. Understanding this figure is a research task in itself. You should look in bookshops (not just specialist photography bookshops), talk to bookshop staff, showing them a copy of your book dummy if at all possible. Ideally you should also talk to sales reps. They will generally be the best placed to understand the breadth of the market. If you have doubts avoid underpricing. Time and inflation should quickly make the book seem cheaper and it is also easier to make good discount offers when you start slightly on the high side. This is particularly important if you intend to concentrate on mail order sales.

grants

Many of the photography books of the last decade would not have been published had they not received funding from the Arts Council.

Barry Lane, Head of Photography at the Arts Council, has been instrumental in the development of mechanisms for the support of book projects. Any photographer considering applying to the Arts Council for publication support would be well advised to discuss their project with him prior to making a submission.

The scheme has a number of key purposes

- To provide viability for short-run book projects

- To enable publishers to achieve high standards of production

- To keep retail prices at a level that makes them accessible to the broadest possible audience

- To encourage an interface between the funded and the commercial sectors

- To provide better equality of opportunity for all photographers

In recent years, and particularly since the restructuring in 1991 of the Regional Arts Associations into Regional Arts Boards, these organisations have begun to look at ways of supporting book publication as one form of support to the "artist".

These new bodies have recognised the importance of the published and broadcast arts and have made key appointments in this area. The title "published and broadcast arts" can, however, be misleading. Many of the officers come from a film background, many transferring from the old RAAs where they were previously film or media officers. Despite variations from region to region, however, it is clear that more attention is being turned to non-literary forms of publishing and that methods of grant-aid support are being developed. Northern Arts , for example, runs a scheme for projects by photographers living or working in the region which offers both grants and loans towards photographic publication.

As someone who believes that publication is an important area of involvement for the visual artist, I have to trust that this trend will continue. Publication in the broadest sense is one of the most effective ways of making the visual arts more accessible to a wide public and is consequently worthy of considerably greater support through public funding policies.

sponsorship

Many photography books are the result of sponsorship. As with most things getting sponsorship is easier said than done. The strategy that I would always adopt is to undertake detailed research prior to making any approach. By this I mean identifying potential sponsors and getting to know as much as you can about the company and their approach to sponsorship. There is little point in firing off letter after letter and receiving nothing back but disappointment. You must find a reason for the sponsorship to be attractive to the company always remembering that true sponsorship is a commercial transaction and the sponsor will be expecting to derive some commercial benefit from their involvement.

Given this, you should approach it as professionally as possible. There is no reason to treat a sponsor any differently than you would treat a publisher who you were trying to persuade to publish your book. Look back at the chapter on "Presenting your work".

Often it is easier to get small amounts of sponsorship from a number of sources rather than to find one single sponsor. Think about how you can split up the costs of your project and consider making approaches based on these elements.

As I have said, be aware of what you can offer in return. Just as an example it might be one of the following

- An exhibition of your work
- A set or part set of prints
- Use of the images for a calendar
- Hosting of the book launch

With any sponsorship that you agree always ensure that the terms are confirmed in writing so that both parties know exactly where they stand. Don't offer more than you can realistically deliver and don't take the money and run. You may well need that sponsor again at some time in the future.

getting the money in

If you take on the role of self-publisher then you take on all the responsibilities of collecting payment.

The quicker you receive payment for any invoice then the less you will be paying out in interest charges to a bank.

- Always send out invoices with the books. Date the invoice for the date of despatch not for the month end and never send just delivery notes followed up by invoices later.

- Make sure that the invoices are as clear as possible. Include full details of the purchase and an order number and name if these have been given by the purchaser. If you give full information now there should be no later clarification needed and therefore no excuse for a delay in payment.

- Allow a sensible credit period. Thirty days is standard. There is little point in saying that your credit terms are 14 days. This will just be ignored.

- It is tempting to offer better terms for early payment – perhaps an additional discount. The problem with this is that many people will take the extra discount but won't necessarily pay you any earlier. It is never easy to get back discount from a customer who shouldn't have taken it. People will also have a variety of tricks such as making out the cheque date within the extra discount period and then claiming postal delays.

- Establish a policy for dealing with late payment. I would suggest that statements be sent out every month and that seven days after payment is due and has not been received a phone call is made to the customer. Always script your conversation. Keep it short and simple –

" This is x. I'm phoning about our invoice 212 which was due for

payment on x. Could you tell me when we will receive your cheque?"

Try if possible to get the name of the person that you are talking to.

- When you have made the phone call send a written reminder confirming the conversation and the date agreed for payment.

If you still don't receive payment then you have to decide whether or not to send a final reminder or to begin the process of debt collection. Many people think of the final reminder as a solicitor's letter. This is unnecessary as generally the most cost-effective way of chasing debt is through the Small Claims Court.

A final reminder might run something along these lines

Dear

We are disappointed that despite previous reminders the sum of £x due as payment for the following invoices still remains unpaid.

Date	Invoice Number	Amount
12/2/92	56983	12.95

Unless we receive payment from you within seven days of the date of this letter we will have no option but to take appropriate legal action to recover this amount. This may result in you being liable to court costs as well as the sum outstanding.

Yours sincerely

a few words of caution

Most short run photography books will not make a profit. It is foolish to try to use a budget to persuade yourself otherwise. Use the budget realistically so that you will be able to understand the likely financial outcome and act accordingly. I think it is far better to go into publication knowing that it is going to cost you £2000 than to pretend to yourself that it will break even.

A final word of monetary caution. Remember that books do not sell themselves. If you are unwilling or unable to put sufficient effort into the sales process you should not proceed. Self-publishing needs real commitment and energy and is not something to be undertaken lightly.

bits and pieces

copyright

Copyright is a complex subject and one that provokes great debate and great confusion. For the purposes of this book I will cover it briefly but for anyone working as a photographer or in any creative capacity it is important to consider the implications of copyright in a broader way than simply its relationship to publishing. I have suggested further reading in the bibliography.

In this country you do not need to register copyright. The very act of creation signifies its existence. Essentially copyright is a form of property – an intellectual or creative property. It must, however, have a tangible substance – an idea or a concept can not be copyrighted. Equally if an idea is turned into something substantive then it is not the idea that is copyright but the object. This may be words or pictures but it can not be thoughts.

Copyright can be bought and sold like any other property. In most instances an author or photographer will assign their copyright to a publisher for the purposes of publication. This is rather like renting out a shop. Ownership is not transferred but the person who rents the shop is allowed to use it to generate income. The rental agreement may also allow them to sub-let part of it to be used by others – again generating income.

As a general rule never sell your copyright always assign it. With a publisher the normal arrangement is that copyright is assigned for an agreed period, often for the full term of the copyright. In this country copyright lasts for fifty years after death and consequently copyright will often pass to other members of the family unless it has previously been sold.

A royalty is the normal method of payment to the copyright owner for the use of the copyright. Royalties are generally set at a percentage of the retail price of a book. The publisher may also sub-license the book for use by others – perhaps for translation into a foreign language or for presentation as a video. There are an immense range of possibilities which you will find described under the section on rights.

The familiar copyright symbol – © – provides protection under international law. It should be followed by the name of the copyright holder. The date of the publication should also be given. The publisher will also normally exert a copyright. This reflects the presentation of the book – its typesetting, layout etc – and is distinct from the content.

Permission to use copyright material should always be sought. If you wish to include a quote or use someone else's photograph then track down the copyright holder and get their agreement. Fees are dependent on the type of use anticipated and the geographical area and often no charge will be made if the proposed book is to have a limited print run.

the copyright libraries

Anyone who publishes a book in the UK is required by law to deposit a copy at each of the six copyright libraries. These are:

The British Library
Legal Deposit Office
Boston Spa, Wetherby, West Yorkshire LS23 7BY

National Library of Wales
National Library of Scotland
Trinity College Library, Dublin
Bodleian Library, Oxford
Cambridge University Library

The copy to the British Library should be sent direct to the address above whilst the other five copies should be sent to

The Copyright Libraries Agency
100 Euston Street, London NW1 2HQ.

Whilst the expense of doing this may be annoying it is good to think that at least six copies of your book should be available for interested readers in a hundred years time.

tax

You should never forget that in publishing a book you are entering into a business activity, and given that it is one that may well lose money you should use every strategy available to you to reduce that loss to the absolute minimum.

If you are not registered as self-employed you should advise the Inland Revenue of your project. This is best done through an accountant, who will help you to avoid the pitfalls and ensure that you get the tax deductions to which you are entitled. At its most basic you should do the following

- Keep records of everything. Buy a small cash book and make sure that you record all costs incurred and keep the receipts. You should start by entering the cost of this book – it should be tax deductible.

- When you are close to beginning to incur large expenditure you should open a separate bank account. It is amazing how complex it can be separating out business and personal costs through a single account.

An accountant will also be able to advise you with regard to VAT. It may be sensible for the self-publisher to become VAT registered. At present the VAT rate on the sale of books is Zero Rate. This means that you will have no VAT liability on the income from the sales of the book itself though you will have to charge VAT on any postage and packing charge that you make to customers.

However you will have to pay VAT for many of the costs associated with the production of the book. These might include the following

Designers' fee
Typesetting
Advertising
Publicity leaflets
Launch costs
Photographic prints

If you are registered then you should be able to reclaim the VAT paid on anything which is a true business expense relating to your book. With VAT currently at 17.5% this would mean that if you had £3,500 of VAT-inclusive expenditure then you should be able to reclaim some £500 of VAT.

Normally there are turnover levels before you need to be VAT registered but you can apply for voluntary registration. One of the reasons generally accepted is that if you were not to be registered you would be put at a commercial disadvantage to others in the same area of work. Clearly if a registered publisher can reclaim £500 that an unregistered one can not there is a commercial disadvantage for the unregistered publisher. The VAT question is best dealt with by an accountant. It is complex and if you do become registered you are required to keep proper books. But, as you should be doing this anyway, keeping the VAT side up to date should not be too much of an added burden.

remaindering

When a book is remaindered it is removed from a publisher's list and offered to specialist remainder merchants who will then seek to sell it on as a bargain book. Once the decision to remainder is taken the pricing of the book does not have to comply with the Net Book Agreement.
Remaindering is done for a number of reasons:

- sales have almost totally died
- high warehousing costs
- shortage of warehouse space
- stock has suffered damage
- to keep the backlist at a manageable size.

Most publishers have some sort of remaindering policy.

It is never very good for the ego to see your book on the remainder shelves but it is something that is increasingly common practice and undertaken at a much earlier stage than previously. There are many publishers who will begin considering remaindering even as soon as twelve to eighteen months after publication. Remaindered books are sold at a fraction of their retail price – less than £1 for a £9.95 book would not be unusual. Remaindering doesn't therefore make much money but it does clear the decks.

You should always ensure that in any contract with a publisher you have first option to buy any stock of your book due to be remaindered. You are likely to be offered copies at a very silly price. Many photographers who have taken up this option have then been able to sell copies at a reduced price but at one that gives them a significant profit and certainly a much better return than they were getting through royalty payments.

international standard book numbers (ISBNs)

ISBNs are available free of charge from:

The ISBN Agency
Whitaker & Sons Ltd
12 Dyott Street, London WC1A 1DF

You should send for an ISBN as soon as you know the title of your book. If you are going to publish more than one title then it is sensible to ask for a block of numbers which you can then allocate yourself to titles as and when they are needed. There is a small charge for this.

ISBNs are important in that they are unique numbers so that any book can be traced from its ISBN.

bar codes

A bar code is a machine-readable code increasingly used by book-shops for stock control purposes. Ideally all books should display a bar code, most usually on the back cover. The bar code symbol includes the ISBN; inclusion of the price is optional. Some of the larger bookshops may be unwilling to stock books which do not have a bar code – so be warned!

There are a number of bar code suppliers. Usually the easiest way to arrange one is to ask your designer or printer to do it on your behalf.

books in print

Whitaker's Books in Print is produced by the same company. This is a full list of books published in UK and is the key information source for bookshops. Standard forms are available from Whitakers which when completed will be entered in BIP free of charge. Whitaker's also publish "The Bookseller" which is the main journal for the book trade.

cataloguing in publication (CIP)

You will have noticed that many books carry library catalogue information. It used to be necessary to approach the British Library to arrange this. Now, thankfully, as long as you have completed your Whitakers standard form all you need to do is include a line on the copyright details page (title page verso) as follows:

A catalogue record for this book is available from the British Library

british book news

This is produced by the British Council which takes an active role in promoting British books overseas. Information on new books is included in BBN free of charge.

British Book News
65 Davies Street, London W1Y 2AA

other useful addresses

Department of Trade and Industry
Dean Bradley House
52, Horseferry Road, London SW1P 2AG

The Fairs and Promotion Branch provides some grants for companies wishing to attend trade fairs abroad.

The Publishers Association
19, Bedford Square, London WC1A 2DF
071 836 8911

The trade body for the publishing industry. Has a very good information service available to members. Also a good source of information on trade fairs. Subscription is quite reasonable for small publishers.

ABSA
Nutmeg House
60 Gainsford Street, Butlers Wharf, London SE1 2NY
071 378 8143

It is well worth contacting ABSA – The Association for Business Sponsorship of the Arts – if you have a particular sponsorship idea in mind. Regional offices have recently been opened.

the funding bodies

Arts Council of Great Britain
14 Great Peter Street, London SW1P 3NQ
071 333 0100

Arts Council of Northern Ireland
18a Stranmillis Road, Belfast BT9 5DU
0232 381591

Welsh Arts Council
Holst House
Museum Place, Cardiff CF1 3NX
0222 394711

Scottish Arts Council
12 Manor Place, Edinburgh EH3 7DD
031 226 6051

regional arts boards

Eastern Arts
Cherry Hinton Hall
Cherry Hinton Road, Cambridge CB1 4DW
0223 215355

East Midlands Arts
Mountfields House
Forest Road, Loughborough, Leics LE11 3HU
0509 218292

Greater London Arts
Coriander House
20 Gainsforth Street, Butler's Wharf, London SE1 2NE
071 403 9013

Northern Arts
10 Osborne Terrace, Newcastle upon Tyne NE2 1NZ
091 281 6334

North West Arts
12 Harter Street, Manchester M1 6HY
061 228 3062

Southern Arts
19 Southgate Street, Winchester, Hampshire SO23 7EB
0962 55099

South East Arts
10 Mount Ephraim, Tunbridge Wells, Kent TN4 8AS
0892 515210

South West Arts
Bradnich Place, Gandy Street, Exeter EX4 3LS
0392 218188

West Midlands Arts
82 Granville Street, Birmingham B1 2LH
021 631 3121

Yorkshire Arts
Glyde House
Glydegate, Bradford BD5 OBQ
0274 723051

glossary

AI sheet – a one-sided sheet giving advance information on a title.

'A' paper sizes – a standard range of paper sizes. AO size is one metre square. When this is folded in half it becomes A1 which when folded again becomes A2 etc. See the reference section for sizes.

ASCII – a standard computer code which enables information exchange between different software programmes.

Backlist – older titles that are still in print.

Blad – usually a printed section of a book used for publicity purposes or for encouraging co-edition interest. It will generally also have a printing of the cover wrapped around and be stapled together.

Blocking – the process used to print the lettering on the cloth binding of a book. Usually a gold or silver foil is used but ink can also be used.

Bulking – using a thicker paper so that a book appears more substantial.

Bar code – a machine-readable code which is increasingly important to bookshops to allow them to maintain electronic stock control. Always use a bar code.

Blurb – usually refers to the text which is used on the back cover to sell the book.

Bleed – where the image goes to the edge of the page. A bleed may be to all or some of the edges. An allowance of 3mm overlap is needed for a bleed. This means that the image will be slightly cropped at any edge where there is a bleed.

Book block – the complete inside of the book with the sections sewn together but prior to the covers being fixed on.

Caps – capital letters.

Cased/Casebound – a hardback binding.

cl – clothbound.

Chromalin – a proofing process for colour images which is intended to simulate the printed result.

Coated paper – paper which has been coated to improve its printing qualities.

Colour separation – the splitting of the image into the four process colours with which it will be printed. These are yellow, magenta, cyan and black.

Copy – text to be typeset.

Copyright – the rights, exclusive to the creator of a work, to reproduce or allow that work to be reproduced.

Cover – paperbacks have covers, hardbacks have jackets.

CRC/Camera ready copy – artwork which is at a finished stage and ready for reproduction.

Crop marks – marks on bromide/film to indicate to the printers/finishers/binders the cutting lines for the page size.

DPS/Double-page spread – a pair of facing pages.

Duotone – two half-tones are produced from a single image by making negatives at different screen angles and with different contrast ranges. This improves the mid-range tones considerably and increases the sense of depth and detail in the image.

Em(s) – printer's/typesetter's term for the measurement of text, based originally on the width of a lower case 'm'. Also known as a pica, it is equivalent to 4.22mm. This text is set across 27.5ems.

Endpapers – generally used in hardbacks and occasionally in softbacks. They have a decorative and functional purpose, providing some strengthening to ensure that the book block is held securely.

Extent – the length of a book expressed in number of pages.

F & Gs – printed sheets folded and guillotined so that they form an unbound version of the finished book.

Facsimile – an exact copy.

Firm sale – an unconditional sale to a bookseller. Generally however publishers will under certain circumstances allow booksellers to return stock for credit. It is very much a decision based on establishing and maintaining goodwill.

Flat sheets – printed sheets which are being held for binding at a later stage.

Folio – a printed page number.

Font (Fount) – originally a printer's term for an individual typeface in one size; now more generally refers to a family of typefaces. This typeface is from the New Caledonia family.

Format – description of a book in terms of its size or shape or in terms of its binding; for example a landscape format is a horizontally shaped book.

Four-colour process – the reproduction of colour photographs. The image is separated into the three primary colours – cyan, magenta and yellow – and black. Each colour is printed with a separate plate.

Frontispiece – an illustration opposite the title page.

Gsm – the weight in grammes of one square metre of the paper. Whilst it is a general guide to thickness it is misleading in that different papers have different qualities. Lower weight papers can appear bulkier.

Galleys – text proofs output from an imagesetter in a continuous roll for eventual cutting and pasting up as the finished artwork. Not used as frequently now as most text is set as pages.

Gutter – the inside margins of a book, ie across the spine; alternately the space between two columns of text.

Gutter spread – where an image runs across a double page.

Half-title – the first printed page of the book or more generally a page which contains just the title of the book.

Half-tone – all printing of images use a dot structure to build up the image. A half-tone is an illustration or photograph which has the effect of a continuous tone created through the use of various sized dots.

Hickeys – small marks, usually spots, on the printed sheet which are the result of dirt, paper dust etc on the plate whilst printing. Care should be taken to remove these quickly as they can spoil an otherwise perfect print.

House style – standard rules chosen by the publisher to achieve a consistency of style in typography and/or grammar.

ISBN – International Standard Book Number. Every book should be allocated an ISBN. This is a unique number enabling the book to be tracked down simply from quoting it.

ISSN – International Standard Serials Number. Used as with books but for magazines and periodicals.

Imposition – the arrangement of pages on the printing plate so that when the printed sheet is folded the pages will run in the correct sequence.

Justification – the setting of text to fill the designated measure without any ragged edges, left or right. This text is justified.

Keyline – a thin line drawn on the artwork to show the exact size and positioning of the image. It may or may not be printed.

Lamination – a thin plastic film usually applied to book covers and jackets. This provides protection and can be either gloss or matt.

Landscape – shorthand for saying that the book (or image) is wider than it is high.

Leading – the spacing between two lines of text, usually measured in points. This text has a leading of 13pts.

Limp binding – a binding with a flexible cover. It usually refers to paperback.

Make ready – the time needed to prepare the printing press to the point where a satisfactory print can be achieved.

Matt – non-glossy, also known as 'dull' in the States.

Mechanicals – finished artwork ready for reproduction.

Overs – copies of a book additional to the number ordered. The publisher is liable to buy these if they are within the following standard tolerances: 5% for single colour work and 10% for colour work. Duotone is considered as colour work.

Ozalid – a low-cost paper proof taken from film prior to plate-making. This allows a check to be made on placing and on the copy. It is not a guide to print quality.

Page – one side only.

Pagination – the page numbering in a book.

Pbk – paperback.

Perfect binding – a deceptive term in that it is not the best form of binding. The pages are glued in rather than sewn.

Plates – 1 photographs or illustrations in a book.
               2 the surface from which the printing is done on press.

Point size – the size of a typeface; a point is one twelfth of a pica or em. This text is set in 11pt.

POS (Point of sale) – promotional material designed to be displayed wherever purchases are to be made.

Portrait – shorthand for saying that the height of the book (or image) is greater than its width.

Prelims (Preliminaries) – the introductory pages of a book before the text or the images start. Includes half-title, title page etc.

Pro forma invoice – an invoice sent out before despatch of the goods.

Progressives – proofs that show each colour individually and then together.

Proof – 1 the checking of typesetting for accuracy.
         2 a test or trial sheet to allow the checking for colour balance, quality of reproduction etc.

Ragged right (or left) – a typesetting term used to describe setting where the left hand edge of the the text is aligned (justified) whilst the right hand edge is not. Page 4 (the verso) is set ragged right.

Ranged right (or left) – the side to which text setting presents a straight edge. Page 4 (the verso) is set ranged left.

Recto – the right hand page of a book. Remember right hand pages are always odd numbers.

Register – the exact positioning and alignment of each colour in the printing process. This should always be checked on press using a strong magnifying glass.

Registration marks – guide marks (usually a cross over a small circle) to ensure that, when printing involves more than one plate, accurate positioning can be achieved.

Repro – the process of turning artwork and photographs into the film required to make printing plates.

Reversal – text or images are reversed out of a black (or other solid colour) so that they print as white. Also known as a WOB (white on black).

Running head – a headline placed at the top of the page and generally repeated across a number of pages, a chapter title for example.

Saddle-stitch – a cheap binding with wire staples holding the pages.

Sale or return – books are invoiced at the end of an agreed period. The bookseller may return any unsold copies and will not be invoiced for these.

Section – each printed sheet when folded and trimmed forms one section of a book.

See safe – books are invoiced on delivery but may be returned for credit.

Sewn binding – any binding in which the sections are sewn together.

Signature – an alternative name for a section.

Self-cover – generally using the first and last pages of a brochure to form the cover and thus using the same material.

Self-ends – using the first and last pages of a book for pasting down to the cover-boards.

Sheet-fed – a printing press that uses paper in separate sheets.

Spine – when books are placed upright on shelves only the spine is visible. It is usually printed with the book title and with the names of both the publisher and the author.

Subscribe – when sales reps try to take orders for a book before it is published it is known as subscribing.

Swatch – samples of paper or binding materials.

Tint – using a percentage density of a colour for an effect.

Trade discount – the discount given to booksellers, wholesalers etc.

Typeface – the style of lettering chosen. There is an immense range, usually sub-divided into serif and sans serif faces. This typeface has serifs (the twiddley bits at the extremities); chapter headings and sub-headings are set in News Gothic, a sans serif face.

Typo – a typographical mistake in the typesetting.

Unders – see Overs. This is the reverse. Always bear in mind the possibility of unders as the tolerance levels of 5% or 10% could result in receiving fewer copies of a book. This can play havoc with the best of budgets.

U/V varnish – a varnish applied to an area (usually an image) and hardened by ultra-violet light. A process undertaken on press.

Varnishing – a process done on press that puts a varnish over areas (usually image areas). It heightens the gloss.

Verso – the left hand page. Generally taken to mean the page on which copyright and other publication details are contained. It is usually directly after the half title page.

further reading

This is a short selection of the many books in print that look at the different aspects of publishing. In addition I would always recommend that considerable time is spent looking at a range of photography books to explore the ways in which design issues have been resolved. There is a lot to be said for looking at the failures as well as the successes. It is often easier to see why something doesn't work. As well as books it is also valuable to look at current design practice in magazines. It is here that you are most likely to find a more adventurous approach to design and layout. Remember though books have a much longer life-span than magazines.

How to Market Books by Alison Baverstock, Kogan Page.
A very thorough and readable guide.

Pocket Pal published by International Paper Company.
Sub-titled "a graphic arts production handbook" this is very useful for those particularly interested in the production side of things.

Publish Your Photo Book by Bill Owens, published by Bill Owens, (USA 1979).
Still worth looking at if you can manage to track down a copy.

Selling Rights by Lynette Owen, Blueprint (1991).
Aimed primarily at the trade. Very good as reference material.

Book Production Practice Publishers Association.
A straight-forward guide to production.

How to Publish Yourself by Peter Finch, Allison & Busby (1987).
Aimed at writers but still a helpful guide.

Inside Book Publishing by Giles N. Clark, Blueprint, (1988)

Offers a good introductory background to the Publishing Industry.

An Author's Guide to Publishing by Michael Legat, Robert Hale (1982 revised 1991).
As it suggests aimed at authors but offering a lot of solid advice on dealing with publishers.

The Booksellers Association Guide to starting and running a bookshop, by M.Breckman, Malcolm Stewart Books (1988).
An excellent way to begin to understand how bookshops operate.

Copy-Editing by Judith Butcher, Cambridge University Press (1992 revised edition)
Because we all make mistakes!

A Code of Practice for Independent Photography by Vince Wade, Artists Newsletter Publications (1989)

Copyright by Roland Miller, AN Publications (1991)

'A' Series

trimmed Sizes	millimetres	inches
A0	841 x 1189	33.11 x 46.81
A1	594 x 841	23.39 x 33.11
A2	420 x 594	16.54 x 23.39
A3	297 x 420	11.69 x 16.54
A4	210 x 297	8.27 x 11.69
A5	148 x 210	5.83 x 8.27
A6	105 x 148	4.13 x 5.83
A7	74 x 105	2.91 x 4.13
A8	52 x 74	2.05 x 2.91

'B' Series

trimmed Sizes	millimetres	inches
B0	1000 x 1414	39.37 x 55.67
B1	707 x 1000	27.83 x 39.37
B2	500 x 707	19.68 x 27.83
B3	353 x 500	13.90 x 19.68
B4	250 x 353	9.84 x 13.90
B5	176 x 250	6.93 x 9.84
B6	125 x 176	4.92 x 6.93
B7	88 x 125	3.46 x 4.92
B8	62 x 88	2.44 x 3.46
B9	44 x 62	1.73 x 2.44
B10	31 x 44	1.22 x 1.73

paper sizes

'C' Series

	millimetres	equivalent in inches	common use
C0	917 x 1297	$36^{1}/_{8}$ x 51	
C1	648 x 917	$25^{1}/_{2}$ x $36^{1}/_{8}$	
C2	458 x 648	18 x $25^{1}/_{2}$	
C3	324 x 458	$12^{3}/_{4}$ x 18	
C4	229 x 324	9 x $12^{3}/_{4}$	takes A4 sheet flat
C5	162 x 229	$6^{3}/_{8}$ x 9	takes A5 sheet flat
C6	114 x 162	$4^{1}/_{2}$ x $6^{3}/_{8}$	takes A5 folded once
C7/6	81 x 162	$3^{1}/_{2}$ x $6^{3}/_{8}$	takes A5 folded twice
C7	81 x 114	$3^{1}/_{4}$ x $4^{1}/_{2}$	
CL	110 x 220	$4^{3}/_{8}$ x $8^{5}/_{8}$	takes A4 folded twice

envelope sizes

Metric Sizes

	8vo		4to	
	mm	*inches*	*mm*	*inches*
Crown	186 x 123	$7^3/_8$ x $4^7/_8$	246 x 189	$9^5/_8$ x $7^1/_2$
Large Crown	198 x 129	$7^3/_4$ x $5^1/_8$	258 x 201	$10^1/_8$ x $7^7/_8$
Demy	216 x 156	$8^1/_2$ x $5^3/_8$	276 x 219	$10^7/_8$ x $8^5/_8$
Royal	234 x 156	$9^1/_4$ x $6^1/_8$	312 x 237	$12^1/_4$ x $9^3/_8$

Imperial Sizes

	8vo		4to	
	mm	*inches*	*mm*	*inches*
Crown	184 x 124	$7^1/_4$ x $4^7/_8$	248 x 187	$9^3/_4$ x $7^3/_8$
Large Crown	197 x 130	$7^3/_4$ x $5^1/_8$	260 x 200	$10^1/_4$ x $7^7/_8$
Demy	216 x 140	$8^1/_2$ x $5^1/_2$	279 x 219	11 x $8^5/_8$
Foolscap	165 x 105	$6^1/_2$ x $4^1/_8$	210 x 168	$8^1/_4$ x $6^5/_8$
Large Post	203 x 130	8 x $5^1/_8$	260 x 206	$10^1/_4$ x $8^1/_8$
Medium	222 x 143	$8^3/_4$ x $5^5/_8$	286 x 225	$11^1/_4$ x $8^7/_8$
Imperial	273 x 187	$10^3/_4$ x $7^3/_8$	375 x 276	$14^3/_4$ x $10^7/_8$

trimmed page sizes – books

centimetres (cm)	cm or inches	inches (in)
2.54	**1**	0.394
5.08	**2**	0.787
7.62	**3**	1.181
10.16	**4**	1.575
12.70	**5**	1.969
15.24	**6**	2.362
17.78	**7**	2.756
20.32	**8**	3.150
22.86	**9**	3.543
25.40	**10**	3.937
50.80	**20**	7.874
76.20	**30**	11.811
101.60	**40**	15.748
127.00	**50**	19.685
152.40	**60**	23.622
177.80	**70**	27.559
203.20	**80**	31.496
228.60	**90**	35.433
254.00	**100**	39.370

conversion table

calculating page sizes

Two examples based on a 720mm x 1020mm sheet size. Not to scale.

8 pages to view

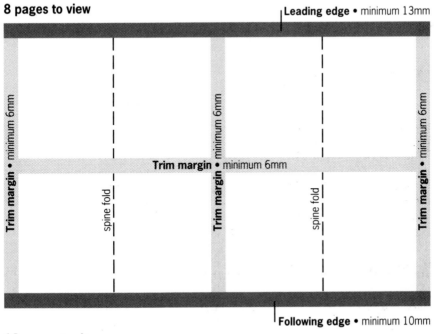

Leading edge • minimum 13mm

Trim margin • minimum 6mm

Following edge • minimum 10mm

12 pages to view

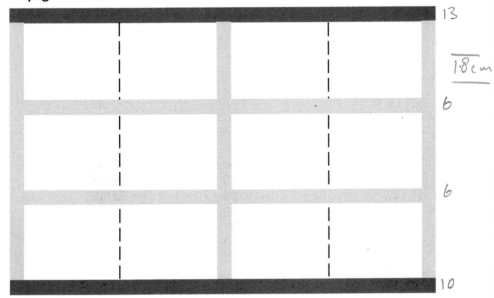

13

1·8cm

6

6

10

35cm

main proofing marks used by printers and designers

Marginal Mark	Text Mark	Meaning
⑦	encircle (words)	check accuracy
⅄	⅄	insert matter in text
⊘	through character/ through ~~the~~ words	delete
⊔⌐	underline	change to italics
≋	under	change to normal caps
⇒	under	change to small caps
⌇⌇	under	change to bold
⊔⌇	under	change to bold italic
≠	encircle characters (TO BE) changed	change caps to lower case
≠	encircle characters (TO BE) changed	small caps to lower case
⊔⊔	encircle (characters) to be changed	change italic to roman
⊙	last word⅃	insert full stop
⌐	word. ⌐Word	start new paragraph
⊣	[Word	indent
⊢	⊢[Word	cancel indent
⊇	last word⌐ ⌐next line	run on text
⊔	wⴋrd	transpose characters
⊂	wo⌒rd	delete space
⋎*	word⋎word	insert space
⋏	word⋏word	reduce space between words

* # is often used as an alternative marginal and text mark

printers

The UK printers with whom we have produced books to date are as follows:

The Alden Press
Osney Mead, Oxford OX2 OEF
Dialogue with Photography   *Publishing Photography*

Balding & Mansell
Park Works, Norwich Road, Wisbech, Cambs TE13 2AX
Broken Images   *Into the Promised Land*
Stones in the Road   *Tony Ray-Jones*

BAS Printers
Over Wallop, Stockbridge, Hants SO20 8JD
Correct Distance   *Ideal Home*

Jackson Wilson
Unit 4 Gelderd Trading Estate, West Vale, Leeds LS12 6BD
The Babies   *Cautionary Tales*
Cheltenham Ladies   *The Cost of Living*
Facing New York   *Furniture Fictions*
A Green & Pleasant Land   *I Can Help*
In Umbra Res   *Looking for Love*
Mike McCartney's Merseyside   *Odd Man Out*
Other than Itself   *The Pleasure Principle*
Presence   *The Red River*
Signs of the Times   *Tradition & Revolution in Russian Art*
Two Blue Buckets   *White Peak, Dark Peak*

H Shanley Ltd
16 Belvoir Street, Tonge Fold, Bolton BL2 6BA
House that Habitat Built   *Sharp Voices, Still Lives*